Public Houses,
Private Lives

An Oral History of Life in York Pubs
in the Mid-20th Century

Mike Race

Published by **Voyager Publications. Tel: 07930 400536**
Published with the support of the **York Oral History Society**

ISBN No. 0 9525392 2 5

Printed by Bullivant and Son, York. Tel: 01904 623241

Cover photograph
Publican Harry Ashton Campbell and his wife Jessie, both on right of picture, and customers outside the York Arms, High Petergate, in the 1930s.

CONTENTS

Members of the women's section of York and District
Licensed Victuallers' Association, as seen by Gay.

Caricatures from The Yorkshire Evening Press, 1940's

INTRODUCTION

The inn, ale-house, tavern, public house, hostelry - call it what you will - has for centuries played a central part in England's social life, and the pivotal figure in the licensed trade is, of course, the licensee. The publican is an individual whose role encompasses manager, social worker, psychologist, comedian, confidante, actor, and bon viveur. He, or she, is often larger than life, tough, tactful, sometimes a hero, sometimes a villain. Much has been written about York's licensed premises but very few writers have touched on, or investigated, the lives of the people who lived and worked in these establishments. One of the exceptions was a Walmgate resident and temperance supporter, Robert Kay, who was vehemently opposed to the licensed trade and whose journal detailing Walmgate pub life in the late nineteenth century, and the excesses and wretchedness that existed, makes fascinating reading. My publication allows publicans and family members the opportunity to tell their stories of life in York's licensed premises in a different era - the mid-20th century.

ACKNOWLEDGEMENTS

Special thanks to the Patricia & Donald Shepherd Charitable Trust for their financial support.

I am extremely grateful to the following for their help in the preparation of this book:

Pauline Worthy for initial help and encouragement; Gill Craddock for carrying out an interview; Ken Law for providing some of the background material; Pauline Coldrick for assisting on interviews and transcribing, and Mrs Hilda Smithson for providing background information and loan of photos. I would like to thank Amanda Howard and the staff of York Reference Library; Rita Freedman and the staff at the City Archives for assistance in research; David Atha for information regarding the Licensed Victuallers Association, loan of photos and supplying contacts; Hugh Murray, John Terry, Bill Stephenson, Joe Gretton, Michael Hannay, Peter Dalton, Pat Hall and Mike Prime for loan of photos; David Poole for supplying historical information and contacts. Finally I wish to thank Van Wilson for her help with interviewing, transcribing and proof-reading, and for her generous advice on matters literary and grammatical .

This book is dedicated to all those interviewed in its preparation. I am grateful to them all for sharing their memories with me, and with you, the reader, and I thank them for the hospitality and generosity shown, without exception, to all the interviewers. Unfortunately Hilda Smithson has died since helping with my research, as have three of the interviewees: Stan Leaf, Doreen Bolton and Eric Shaw. Stan Leaf had a long and varied career as a railwayman, policeman, hotelier and publican. Eric Shaw spent his working life as a mechanic, and had a passion for motorbikes. He was an enthusiastic member of the Eboracum Motorcycle Club in the 1950s, and regularly attended the T.T. Races on the Isle of Man. Doreen Bolton is still remembered among the city's older imbibers as the epitome of a pub landlady – warm, generous, and with an infectious sense of fun.

PROFILES OF THE INTERVIEWEES

Harry Atkins worked part-time as a barman at the York Arms, High Petergate, where his sister and her husband, Kathy and Sid Staines, were the licensees from 1954 to 1976.

Noel Attree was born at the Red Lion in Merchantgate in 1914 and lived there with his grandmother, Christina Davison. Noel stayed at the Red Lion until 1932 before moving to the Woolpack Inn, Fawcett Street, to live with his mother, Gladys – who held the tenancy there from 1918 to 1947 – and his step-father Leonard Darch. Many of Noel's close relations ran pubs in York, including the Market Tavern, Coppergate; the Waggon and Horses, Lawrence Street; the Crown Brewery Hotel in Walmgate and the Coach and Horses, Nessgate.

Bob Barker was born in George Street in 1916 and returned to the area of his birth when he became the tenant at the Brown Cow in Hope Street. He ran the pub with his wife Pam from 1954 to 1976. He combined the tenancy with life in the civil service, and had previous experience in the pub trade when he worked as a barman in the Old Grey Mare in Clifton, in the early 1950s.

Doreen Bolton was born in 1910 and died in Haxby in 1996. She was a member of the Gretton family who had a long tradition of service in the licensed trade in York. Mrs Bolton was, famously, the landlady of the Royal Oak, Goodramgate from 1938 (when she claimed to be the youngest landlady in Yorkshire) to 1950.

Arthur and Eve Briggs' first venture into the licensed trade was in 1951, when they became tenants of the Bay Horse in Marygate. It proved a very successful move, as they built up a good business and stayed there for 35 years, until their retirement in 1986.

Pauline Coldrick's father, Horace, was a rugby-playing Welshman whose first pub was the Waggon and Horses, Gillygate, where Pauline was born and where he was the licensee from 1935 to 1949, except for the war years when his wife Anne took over the reins. The family then moved to the Frog Hall, Layerthorpe, where Mr Coldrick was the tenant until 1973, and where Pauline 'helped out' as a part-time barmaid, as well as having a full-time position with British Rail.

Doug Dalton's father Harold became manager of the Greyhound Hotel, Spurriergate in 1956. On his death in December 1957, his wife Kathleen took over the licence, ably assisted by Doug, who lived with his parents, and with help from his married brother Peter, who later became landlord of the Wellington Inn, Alma Terrace. The Daltons were the last licensees of the Greyhound, which finally shut its door in 1958.

Barbara Fletcher was the long standing landlady of a city centre pub, the Londesbro' Hotel in Petergate, from 1963 to 1976. Mrs. Fletcher gained experience in the licensed trade when she worked at the Golden Lion in Church Street, and later at the Golden Lion in St. Sampson's Square.

Lily Grayson's parents, Bradley and Harriet Gott took the tenancy of the Phoenix Inn, George Street – their first and only pub – in 1931 and stayed there until they retired in 1951. Mrs. Grayson helped out behind the bar and has fond memories of life at the Phoenix.

Barry Grayson came to York in 1976 when he became the landlord of the York Arms in Petergate, a pub which he ran with his wife, Marie, until 1996, a period which saw great changes in the way public houses were run.

Doreen Greaves was brought up at the Pack Horse in Micklegate, where her father Albert Brown was the manager from 1935 up to his death in 1942. His wife Marjorie then took over until her retirement in 1955. Doreen married John Greaves in 1952 and they ran the Lion and Lamb, Blossom Street until their retirement in 1986.

John Greaves was born at the Lion and Lamb in Blossom Street in 1922. His mother was the tenant there from 1905 – with her first husband, Harry Bramfitt, until his death in 1916, and then with her second husband Charles – until 1955, when John and his wife Doreen became the publicans. John was to be the last landlord of the Lion and Lamb. When he retired the pub was refurbished, and after more than 250 years under its previous sign, was renamed 'The Nickel and Dime'. It didn't last – the pub that died of shame?

Betty Harris's first introduction to pub life came when she married her then husband, Don Nixon, in 1956, and lived with her in-laws at the Golden Lion in St. Sampson's Square. She remembers trembling and hating her first day behind the bar, but after taking the tenancy of the Woodman Inn, Bishopthorpe, with her husband Don in 1960, she grew to love the trade, "I was happy, I was proud, I loved it".

Edith Keech's husband Bert was born at the Minster Inn, Marygate, a pub that was tenanted by members of the Keech family for 87 years. Mrs. Harriet Keech, Bert's mother, held the licence herself for almost 52 years, until her death in 1944. Both Bert and Edith helped out behind the bar of the 'Minster' until they took the tenancy of the De Grey Rooms – which then functioned as a restaurant, bar and dance hall – in 1941. After Bert's early death in 1954, Edith continued at the De Grey Rooms until 1963. She then worked at Elliotts Hotel in Sycamore Place, Clifton, retiring in 1998 after working for 60 years in these three establishments.

Stan and Gladys Leaf ran the Phoenix Inn, George Street from 1953 to 1963. Mr Leaf was born in 1905 and died in Heslington in 1996. He worked on the railways and in the police force, and was a hotelier in Whitby before moving to York and taking the tenancy of the Phoenix.

Vera Lyall's first pub was the Pack Horse in Micklegate which she managed from 1956 to 1957, before moving to the Lord Nelson in Walmgate where she held the licence until 1962. Her husband, Tony, then left his employment with the Gas Board and took the tenancy of the Three Cranes Inn, St. Sampson's Square, which he and Vera ran until their retirement in 1979.

Don Nixon's first experience of pub life came as a teenager, when his mother and father took the tenancy of the Golden Lion, St. Sampson's Square in 1950. Don took to the licensing trade 'like a fish to water' and went on to become the landlord of the Woodman Inn, Bishopthorpe from 1960 – 1967, the Blacksmith's Arms, Naburn, 1978 – 1980, and the Castle Howard Ox, Townend Street, 1980 – 1989.

Lela Norfolk came to York from Harrogate in 1955 when her husband, Fred, took the tenancy of the Mount Hotel. Mr. Norfolk died in 1962 but Lela took over the licence and stayed at the Mount until her retirement in 1970.

Judy Plaxton was born in York in 1939, and had her first experience of pub life in 1953 when her father, Cliff Bradley, became manager of the Nag's Head in Heworth. Judy stayed at the Nag's Head until her marriage in 1961, and in 1976 she and her husband, Alan, became publicans in their own right when they became the licensees at the Exhibition Hotel in Bootham, where they stayed until 1984.

Ron Powell was born at the Bay Horse, Blossom Street, in 1921 and lived there until his marriage. His grandfather and father were the tenants, consecutively, from 1909 to 1967. Ron served in the R.A.F. during the Second World War and spent the rest of his working life as an electrician. He was never tempted to carry on the family tradition.

Eric Shaw's parents, Maurice and Lillian, took over the running of the Angler's Arms, Goodramgate in 1929, the year he was born. They stayed as tenants until 1953, when they moved to the Melbourne, Cemetery Road, staying until 1956. Mr. and Mrs. Shaw's final pub was the Beeswing, Hull Road which they kept from 1961 to 1965. Like many publicans' children – who either loved or hated pub life – he had no liking for pubs and never considered a life as a publican. Eric died in Huntington in October 1998.

Gill Thompson was born in Wenlock Terrace and her grandparents were tenants at the Barrack Tavern, Fulford Road. The family later moved to The Edinboro Arms, Fishergate, where her father, Merrick Bousfield, was the landlord from 1958 to 1967. Gill well remembers visits to the pub from many members of the famous pop groups who were appearing at the Rialto during that period.

Fred Veitch was born in 1926 and lived at the Five Lions Hotel, Walmgate, from 1935 when his parents moved there and his father, Peter, became the manager. Although Fred left home in 1943 for navy life, the pub stayed in the family until 1981, Fred's sister Peggy and her husband John Seago taking over the licence on their father's demise.

Sheila White was born at her grandmother's 'off-licence' in Swann Street in 1925, and many of her aunts and cousins had hotels and pubs in York. She and her husband, Jim, first ventured into the licensed trade in 1960 when they took the Ship Inn, King's Street. They also kept off-licenses in Winterscale Street and Walmgate and were tenants at the Jubilee Hotel, Leeman Road, and the Castle Howard Ox in Townend Street, where she spent, "the happiest years of my life" and from where she and her husband retired in 1980.

Joan Whitehead was born Joan Farrington in York in 1925. Her mother, Doris, was the manager of the Three Tuns, Coppergate from 1942 to 1951. After her marriage, Joan and her husband Norman ran the Britannia Inn, Nunnery Lane. They left in 1954 when they became mine hosts at the Spotted Cow Hotel, Barbican Road – where they introduced very popular jazz evenings – and from where they retired in 1981.

Mabel Wilson was born in December 1903, the daughter of Henry Brabbs, a well-known York landlord for more than sixty years, thirty five of them as the licensee of the Albion, Skeldergate. He also kept the Bricklayer's Arms, Hungate; the Red Lion, Micklegate; the Edward V11, Nunnery Lane; and was the first landlord of the Corner House, Burton Stone Lane. Mrs. Wilson spent most of her life prior to her marriage at the Edward V11, which she helped to run after her mother's early death.

Van Wilson's mother and step-father, Moira and Geoff Potter, were tenants of the Britannia Inn, Nunnery Lane, for a short period in the late 1950s. During the same period her maternal grandparents, Alex and Helen McTurk, were the licensees of the White Swan, Goodramgate. Van's mother also 'helped out' at the White Horse, Bootham and the York Arms, High Petergate, when friends of hers were the tenants there. Van's childhood memories of living in and visiting licensed premises are not particularly happy ones, and have left her with a dislike of pub life.

Pauline Worthy's family ran the Talbot Hotel, Church Street from 1922, when her grandfather John Richard Cross became the tenant, until 1957 when her mother retired as the licensee. Pauline was born at the Talbot in 1935, the daughter of Meg and Gilbert Foulkes Heatley. Pauline helped her mother run the hotel when her father died in 1952, and has some lingering regrets at not having continued the family tradition of tenancy at the Talbot.

SETTING THE SCENE – YORK'S PUB HISTORY

Although this publication is essentially an oral history of life in York public houses in this century, I thought it prudent to include the following potted history of the City's inns and taverns. Of course many of these licensed premises have called time forever.

York has always had more than its fair share of licensed premises, providing sustenance not only for its citizens but also the local rural community, the military, and visitors from near and far. In the fifteenth century, foreign visitors to the city were only allowed to lodge at the Bull in Coney Street (the Bull eventually became the George and was demolished in 1868 when Leak and Thorpe built their store on the site). In 1604 an Act of Parliament recognised inns, taverns and alehouses as places 'for the receipt, relief and lodging of Wayfaring People travelling from Place to Place' – however, as many writers of the time record, the appalling conditions prevailing in these places, "fleas so large you could squash them between finger and thumb like new boiled peas" (John Taylor, the Water Poet, on his description of the bedroom at an inn in 1649), one wonders at the quality of the 'relief' provided!

In 1550 only nine inn-holders are recorded in the city but by 1596 there were sixty four inn-holders and 103 ale-house keepers with eighty brewers active. In 1578 all inn-holders were expected to provide at least six beds and minimum fare consisting of pottage, boiled and roast meat and ale or beer. Prices were controlled and brewers were ordered to sell ale at fourpence a gallon, best beer at threepence a gallon and single ale at a penny a gallon. Publicans sold ale at five pence a gallon 'to take away' and six pence when drunk on the premises.

It is the general consensus that the 'Starre' in Stonegate is the longest established hostelry in York, although other premises may have a claim, as little written material concerning medieval inns in York has survived the passage of time, and some of the published information regarding the age of York licensed properties is inaccurate. For instance, most publications state that the former Lion and Lamb in Blossom Street was first licensed in 1798, when in fact the hotel was advertised for sale in the York Courant of 12 May 1789 and was described as 'this ancient inn'.

The City's pubs have always been social centres and before the advent of mass communication were often the places where information, news and opinion were distributed. In the 16th and 17th centuries they were used as unofficial trading centres for merchants and merchandisers, that is until further public house licensing in 1631 allowed the Corporation – who, with the trading guilds were concerned that the trade was threatening the guild's monopoly – to take more control over local hostelries.

Before the days of the railway, York was full of coaching inns, including the George Hotel, Coney Street; the White Swan, Pavement; Etridge's, Museum Street; the White Horse, Coppergate, and the Elephant and Castle in Skeldergate. The Black Swan in Coney Street had stabling for 160 horses, and coaches left for London three days a week, and Liverpool and Newcastle two days a week. One needs little imagination to evoke the scene on the arrival of the London coach – the sweating, gasping horses, their hooves clattering on the courtyard cobbles, the tooting of the guard's horn, the swish of the coachman's whip, the barking dogs and shouting of hurrying ostlers – and the relief on the passengers' faces on safely arriving at journey's end! Travelling by stage-coach was always a hazardous business. In 1708, the diarist and historian Ralph Thoresby wrote, prior to a journey from Leeds, "May 17 – preparing for a journey to York. Lord, grant thy favourable presence from sin and all dangers. We found the way very deep, and in some days very dangerous for a coach (that we walked on foot), but the Lord preserved us from all evil accident, that we got to our journey's end in safety, blessed be God".

The public house has, through history, taken the blame for much of society's ills and problems. In 1599 the Lord Mayor and Aldermen complained of many citizens absenting themselves from church on Sunday, "Lying in their beds, or sitting at their doors or in the street or walking abroad in the fields, or sitting in the ale houses or taverns playing at unlawful games so long as they have money or credit". Further shame was brought on the licensing trade in the eighteenth and nineteenth centuries when, in the expanding industrial cities, the pub became the refuge of the poorer section of society who sought solace from the appalling poverty that engulfed them – but of course added to their destitution in doing so. In the late seventeenth century, Parliament brought in measures that were to have a far reaching effect on the drinking habits of the English: severe taxation of beer, prohibition of foreign spirits and the encouragement of home industries to distil and retail spirits made from British grown corn. This policy was to produce 'gin fever', as imbibers eagerly sought the new, cheap alternative to ale. In 1736 one house in four in London was a gin shop, and Henry Fielding wrote that, "Gin is the principal sustenance (if so it might be called) of more than a hundred thousand people in the Metropolis" – although not in York, where there is very little evidence of wide-spread gin addiction. In 1830 the government sought to reduce spirit consumption by introducing 'beer only' houses, whereby any householder with a house in excess of £10 a year rateable value could sell beer on payment of a two guinea licence fee, and many unsuitable premises were used, bringing more problems with drunkenness rather than less.

In the latter part of the nineteenth and the early part of the twentieth centuries the temperance movement, often with the support of the police, magistrates and Licensing Justices, sought to, and succeeded in, reducing the number of licensed premises in York. In the 100 year period prior to the First World War, 138 public houses closed, leaving only 180 ale and spirit and 32 'beer only' houses licensed in the city. The war produced further problems for the city's landlords when beer sales fell by 25%, despite, during some periods of the hostilities, having in excess of an additional 8,000 troops stationed in the city. This fall was caused by pubs having to close at 9 p.m.; the reduction in beer production nationally from 36 million to 10 million barrels per year; and the imposition of war duty, which increased the price of a pint of beer from 3d to 4d. By 1929 the number of licensed premises in York had dropped to 150 fully licensed and 24 'beer only' houses. This figure remained fairly constant for the next forty years, there being 160 fully licensed houses in the city in 1966.

During Queen Victoria's reign, the emancipation, education and organisation of the working man began in earnest. One of the fruits of this organisation was the formation of the working men's club movement. As an example of the higher aspirations and educational zeal of the time it was announced at a York W.M.C. meeting that, "An elocution class has been formed"! By 1912 there were 38 working men's clubs in York with a total of 6,662 members. This massive membership can be partly explained by the large scale closure of public houses in the city and the refusal of the authorities to grant licensed premises in the expanding inner suburbs.

After the First World War licensed premises gained respectability with most sections of society, and the public house became a place to socialise as well as drink. Even in Victorian times the better regulated and more salubrious premises had been natural meeting places for the city's sportsmen; cricketers, anglers, cyclists and rowers held dinners and meetings at a variety of the local hostelries, and various indoor sports leagues were formed, albeit in small numbers. However by the 1930s dominoes and darts leagues were becoming a regular feature of pub life.

The public house has always been a male bastion, but the contribution of women in successive world wars brought some easing of traditional taboos, and respectable mature ladies could enjoy a discreet drink together in certain better class public houses by the 1920s – although it took the Second World War to finally bring about the freedom for women to visit most York public houses without a male escort – and even then usually feeling comfortable only in groups. By the 1960s, one in four of a pub's customers were women. They were confident enough to run their own games leagues, and the public house has generally become a more decent and comfortable place because of their presence.

The best public houses are continually changing and evolving, but are always aware of the tradition and place they hold in English society. There is evidence that the friendly tenant/landlord of old is being replaced by a less visible and more impersonal manager, a business man, with budgets to meet and targets to aim for. Let's hope that the old concept of service – the landlord's requirement to serve a good pint, sympathise, organise, calm and cheer – and, of course, call, "Time Gentlemen please" – will never be lost.

1. The Publican's Day

The publican's day was a long and busy one, supervising – or carrying out – cleaning, organising bar staff, checking deliveries, meeting company reps., adding up the takings, cellar work, and, of course, serving the customers. Time off for 'good behaviour' was often spent with fellow licensees – licensed victualler's dinners and trips were popular and well attended. In this chapter the landlord or family members describe their work and play, the tasks they performed and the people they dealt with.

Prior to the advent of pressurised beer, 'keeping a good pint' was an essential art of the good landlord. Good beer meant good custom.

1. Reg Heatley pulls a pint of Tetley's beer at the Talbot Hotel, whilst Meg, his wife, watches. 1940s. *(Pauline Worthy)*

Noel Attree: *It was a profession really, to keep a good pint, and it had to be a good pint otherwise you got no trade, they'd send it back straight away* (at the Red Lion, Merchantgate), *even at sixpence a pint. If there was anything ... sometimes there'd be a little bit of something floating about in it, or it wasn't a good top on it, or if it wasn't crystal clear, you know, to look at. No, they wouldn't have that.*

Don Nixon: *The pride was in the presentation of the beer; it had to have a good head on it. If you get a pint that's pulled well, the froth will still be on the top when you've taken the first drink, and after each drink. We used to say, "Old so-and-so, he'll do it in three, and so-and-so, he'll do it in four". With a good pint you can tell how many times that person has put a drink in their mouth. If you keep a good, clean, cool pint, have a good sense of humour, good atmosphere, clean pub, you'll get the people in – whose beer* (it is) *doesn't really matter. It's looking after it that's important.*

Harry Atkins: *It was essential to attract the custom in those days* (the York Arms in the 1950s), *to keep the beer a good quality. You had to watch your cellar management.*

Lela Norfolk: *Oh, it was very ordinary* (at the Mount Hotel) *but they didn't care what discomforts they had as long as the beer was all right. It always had a right good name for a good pint.*

Here publicans talk of the time it took, the difficulties encountered and the skill involved in keeping beer in good condition.

2. Bob Barker behind the bar of the Brown Cow, Hope Street. c.1970.   *(Bob Barker)*

Bob Barker: *There is an art in keeping beer. Every night when I'd finished* (at the Brown Cow), *I used to drain off all the pipes and put cleaning fluid in, every night, never missed. And before I went to work I used to draw clear water before I put the beer on, and I emptied them every night. And on Sunday I had a real go, you know. I used to swill out the cellar and then dismantle the pumps, taking 'em down and putting the sponges through and everything – you used to put a sponge in the bottom of the pipe, and when you drew the water up it came right to the top of the pump – then you dismantle it.*

John Greaves: *We used to get a delivery on a Tuesday* (at the Lion and Lamb), *you know, the real ale. We would put it on the gantries and never look at it 'til Friday or Saturday, because it needed time to settle. Then if it didn't settle entirely you could get what you called 'finings', which were made from fish bones, and you would mix that with some beer and pour it in and it would take all the sediment down. But it takes longer than the modern keg beer which was already...well clear really. On some barrels in the old days you used to get a tremendous amount of 'silage' – the stuff that settled down, it did take longer, yes. The other thing, the main thing I think, whatever they did, basically, was having clean equipment. If you didn't clean the pipes, or if your pipes were warm, you'd get a sort of haze on the beer, you know. This was a problem, but these days it's all refrigerated and sanitised, so there's quite a bit of difference I suppose. In those days the barrels were all wooden ones, and occasionally you'd get a leak in a barrel, and we used to seal it with brown paper. If you put brown paper in and tapped it with a gantry chock, the thin end, you could knock the brown paper in and seal it. There were all sorts of little tricks.*

Betty Harris: *There was a huge art in it; you had to know when to stop a barrel. Don would tilt it, he'd put the chocks under it, go to a darts match, and say, "Listen, another ten pints, knock that one off and go onto another one". We had no refrigeration at the Woodman, so on hot days there was only one way to cool the beer down – hosepipe. Run the hosepipe up and down, and wet sacks. It was all hand pulled, wooden casks. None of this canister stuff.*

3. Betty and Don Nixon outside the Woodman, Bishopthorpe, in the early 1960s.

(Betty Harris)

12

Sheila White: *I learnt my cellar work from my cousin who had the Crown in Micklegate, Jack Goodrick. After I learnt the cellar work he taught Jim* (her husband) *how to do it, and he's an excellent cellar man is Jim. His beer was always good. He did his husbandry very well; on the night, every night he used to put water through the pumps. He used to ask,"Anyone want anymore?" and then he'd go down into the cellar, he'd switch off, he'd put the pipes into the water, pull off the old beer, pull through the water and he used to leave them to soak overnight. And he used to pull it off next morning and start from scratch. He always kept his pipes clean. If you went into his cellar it was like a milk dairy, with everything laid out, like a doctor lays all his instruments out. And he allus' got top marks for cellar work, and his cellar never went above 55, and that's correct – now they freeze the guts out of beer, but years ago the correct cellar temperature was 55 degrees, and now it can be anything to minus. In those days the beer had to stand for a couple of days to settle it. Whereas now, today, you just take the cans, the cans are in the cellar, take a barrel off and put a new one on in about two minutes and you're back in service. With the old type of beer that had a lot of finings and things, you had to wait while it settled, otherwise it could be cloudy and people wouldn't buy it. There was a lot of skill, you've got to put hard pegs in and soft pegs and ease them out. If you've got a barrel of Bass, you can spile it* (fix a wooden peg in the top of the barrel) *tap it, put the tap in, put the spile in and it'll hit the ceiling because it's so lively. There's a way of doing it. Or you can tap it and if you don't hit it with the bung right, you lose half of it, because once you've hit the bung, you can't take it out again, otherwise it'll express itself.*

Barry Grayson: *The art is simple: the beer was brought in, they were racked by the draymen, and you left them. You tapped and spiled them, and then you left them until you wanted to use them, and you cleaned your pipes religiously. That's the art – you keep your pipes clean, and you don't disturb.*

If you lived near the River Ouse, keeping your beer undisturbed could sometimes be a problem.

Doug Dalton: *The cellar was like something out of the dark mysterious past* (at the Greyhound Hotel in Spurriergate). *The higher the Ouse rose, the more water we got in the cellar. Horrendous. One very, very, cold February we'd had one of York's typical ex–winter floods. My father said, "Will you go down and change a barrel?" And I went down these steps, the lower I went, the higher the water came up. And before I got into my wellingtons I thought, "This is silly". So my father said, "Put your swimmimg costume on and have a go down there". So I went down, and the water was over waist high. And to my horror there were barrels literally bouncing about at the end of the pipes in the water. And they'd got themselves tangled up – from one side they'd come across to the other. I always* *remember, it was a hell of a job sorting out which pipe belonged to which barrel, mixing the bitter up with the mild. And I came out of that cellar very, very, cold indeed. And there were some people in the bar, I don't know what they thought, me coming up behind the bar with a pair of swimming trunks on, mother standing there with a huge towel to put round me.*

4. Harold and Kathleen Dalton at the Greyhound Hotel, Spurriergate. 1957. *(Peter Dalton)*

There was also a skill in serving bottled beers:

Don Nixon: *Pour on the thumb. You put your hand round the glass, pour on the thumb. I used to hold with the left, pour with the right. Now you automatically tilt the glass, and the first thing you see on the side of the glass is your thumb. And as the beer gets to the thumb, which is well below the top, you straighten it up and pour the rest in.*

Noel Attree: *You had to be careful with bottled Bass, 'cos there was sediment in the bottom, you had to pour it very gently. There was an art in it actually, in leaving the sediment behind, and not getting any in the glass.*

The working day was long and didn't always end when the last customer had gone.

Eric Shaw: *They* (his parents at the Angler's Arms) *never left cleanin' up 'til the next day. They preferred to go to bed at one, half past one in the morning and maybe not get up 'til nine. Did it that way, rather than get up and clean a mucky pub. The only other bit of cleanin' that ever happened was me mother on her hands and knees, white stoning t'step. She did that every morning with a scrubbin' brush. She had a block of white stone and she'd stone all t'step every morning. Other than that they did it all on a night when they finished. Me dad did the cellar work before he opened in a morning, saw to all t'barrels and that. He meticulously cleaned his pumps – he used to pull hot water and soda through, then clear water, and clean 'em out. He had four pumps and he cleaned them out at least once a week. That's how it was, they never employed anybody, they just ran it themselves.*

5. Maurice Shaw at the Angler's Arms, Goodramgate. 1940s.   *(Eric Shaw)*

6. A dinner function held in the ballroom of the De Grey Rooms. c.1950.

(Edith Keech)

Gladys Leaf: *In the passage way* (at the Phoenix) *we had coconut matting there, with the farmers making a mess. When they'd all gone and before I went to bed we used to roll it up, take it into the street and shake it and mop up . . . oh dear.*

Lela Norfolk: *We used to give the old cellar a good swill out at two and three in a morning. It didn't matter.*

Edith Keech: *I really wonder how I did it* (running the bar, restaurant and dance hall at the De Grey Rooms) *because we didn't get to bed 'til half past two, three o'clock, because there was dancing 'til two, and then I was up about seven o'clock – there were letters to see to and the phone and one thing and another. We led a very busy life.*

Before licensing laws became more restrictive the working day would start in the early morning:

Mabel Wilson: *We were at the Edward VII all the war* (the First World War), *and that was quite an experience. In those days men used to go to work at six in the morning and the bar used to be open for rum and coffee, before they went. Either my father was up or my mother was up to let them in. The men used to come in either going or coming off work for a rum and coffee in the morning, and there was many an amount of time wasted – they didn't get to work with them having too much.*

Noel Attree: *Used to open while six in a mornin' – from about five 'til six. In cold weather you could get a rum and coffee, I can just remember that. That was goin' on nearly eighty years ago – a long time . . . that would be just after the First World War – maybe durin' First World War for all I know.*

And of course the licensing hours weren't always strictly adhered to!

Joan Whitehead: *We used to start at seven in a morning* (cattle market day at the Spotted Cow), *that was unofficial of course . . . tea, coffee, whisky and rum – wouldn't sell any beer that time in a morning. The official opening hours were eleven to four and half past five while eleven. But we never used to stop, used to go right through, work right through, just shut front door and open the back door.*

Judy Plaxton: *They were all drinkin'* (after hours at the Nag's Head) *when somebody shouted, "Police is outside!" and they banged and they brayed and me dad let 'em in, and everybody had run upstairs, and they were in the bathroom, wardrobes – everywhere. And George* (a customer) *was getting over t'wall to go to his cottage, and he was so big he couldn't get over fast enough. And policeman said to him, "Where are you goin'?" and he said, "I'm goin' home". They got away with it. My dad said he was having a party for one of us, so they got away with it.*

Fred Veitch: *Irishmen used to come there on a Sunday morning* (at the Five Lions) *beggin' to be sold a pint of beer, you know, maybe nine or ten o'clock – 'a hair of the dog' they called it in those days – they'd maybe stand at the back door and me dad would serve 'em. There was no trouble though, they would drink it down and they'd be back at twelve o'clock. He got caught once; pubs used to shut at half past two and you got people waiting for their bus – wasn't maybe 'til four o'clock – and they would just stop in, if there were any customers about you were glad to get 'em. I allus remember the magistrate saying to him, "If ever I have to wait for a bus, I know where to come!"*

Arthur Briggs: *We were always having 'lock ins'* (at the Bay Horse, Marygate). *Every Saturday night, they used to ring bloody bell at midnight. They used to leave the Sergeants' Mess at Fulford and come round.*

Lela Norfolk: *You had to make your money somehow* (by allowing customers to stay drinking after hours). *It was a bit dangerous, 'cos you know where the Mount Hotel was – you're close to the town. I think they* (the police) *knew. So long as you weren't rowdy or noisy – no trouble – they didn't bother you. They didn't seem to bother us.*

7. The Golden Lion and Duke's Bros. fish and chip shop, St. Sampson's Square. 1950s.
(City of York Archives)

Don Nixon: *Quite a number of people, especially* (market) *stall holders, would come across at four o'clock, half past four, in the afternoon – used to come in through the back door* (at the Golden Lion, St. Sampson's Square, in the 1950s). *And after they'd had a few pints they used to nip next door when the fish shop opened, and get themselves some fish and chips, and then come back and get a few drinks.*

The breweries expected their pubs to be open no matter what the family circumstances.

John Greaves: *I remember when my mother died, at the same time, the same day, Doreen was in hospital, but I daren't close. You daren't close your pub or they'd want to know why. That same evening – I think it was a Saturday – I had two coach loads in from Leeds, full of beer, they'd been to the coast, and I thought, "God this is all I need, I've got the treble up now".*

Pauline Coldrick: *My mother had a heart attack on the Sunday night, we got her to hospital and she died early hours Monday morning. He* (her father at the Frog Hall) *had the pub open at eleven o'clock on the Monday, he daren't do otherwise. That was your licence, and that was in 1962.*

Joan Whitehead: *You could get into trouble if you didn't open. One time you couldn't even close for a funeral. If there was a death in the family, you couldn't close a pub.*

However, by the 1980s a more 'free and easy' attitude to opening was beginning to emerge, and landlords were sometimes reluctant to open their doors to just one customer. The old standards and disciplines were beginning to erode:

Arthur Briggs: *Later on, on a dinner time, on a bad day, I'd shut door, I'd close at one. If someone came knocking at t'door, I'd say, "We're closed, there's a pub at top of t'hill".*

A landlady had to 'look the part' when she was serving customers, but there were other jobs to be done, and it wasn't always possible to be glamorous!

Eve Briggs: *When we first went in I used to scrub on my knees every morning, you know, that big hall, all the jug and bottle steps, the great big front steps, the toilets – 'cos it was all tiled floors. One day – you know you wore a turban when you were working – I was scrubbin' the hall, and this beautiful car pulled up outside. He said, "Excuse me, is the proprieter in?". And I said, "Just a minute sir, I'll go and get him", making him think that I'm the cleaner. He comes out* (her husband) *and he says, "Have you met my wife?" 'Cos at night I was so glammed up, it wasn't true. I could have killed him! Murdered him!*

Doreen Bolton: Landladies night out, we all used to go. I always remember Lil. Shaw, (the landlady of the Anglers Arms) *she had two fox furs and a hat with flowers on. And we'd had one or two like, and I used to say to Lil just before we got there* (to the Anglers Arm's on their way home), *"Get furs off before you get in, they might be fallin' in t'hot water". And as we opened t'door there was t'mop and bucket with steam comin', ready for her to mop up.*

Running a pub was often a family affair, and family members were expected to pull their weight in serving customers and keeping the premises clean:

8. Eve Briggs at the Bay Horse, Marygate. 1970s.
(Eve and Arthur Briggs)

Barbara Fletcher: *I had two sons who used to help me to do t'pipes, twice a week we used to do them* (at the Londesbro' Hotel). *The five girls, as they grew up they all worked for me, and it was a laugh a minute. As they grew older it was beneficial, 'cos they helped out and I sat back a little then.*

Doreen Greaves: *My mother used to say* (at the Pack Horse), *"Fetch us some Guinness our Doreen". I used to lift two dozen at a time, Guinness, and we used to put 'em near the fire so that they wouldn't starve to death, so they'd be ready to drink.*

Eric Shaw: *And then as I got older . . . I was stocking up the beer bottles that were under the counter. So I'd bring crates in, empty 'em and stock up with bottles and whatnot. There were spittoons in the bar, I used to have to clean these out on a morning. I used to have to get t'spittoons when the old lads had finished smokin' their pipes and chewin' their black shag and all this carry on. Rake it into an ash tin, wash 'em out, then we'd fill 'em with fresh sawdust again and put 'em back in t' bar.*

9. Landlady Barbara Fletcher and daughters Mandy, Maxine, Marilyn, Maureen and Jean at the Londesbro' Arms, Petergate. 1970s. *(Barbara Fletcher)*

Mabel Wilson: *And in the public bar there were spittoons, enamel filled with sawdust, and then in the others it was brass ones, and we used to have to do them every day. Every Friday was barrel washing day, we used to take it in turns, the barmaid and me, to draw all the water through the pipes while father was downstairs cleaning them. It was a real day's hard work, but you got used to it. And for all I was the landlord's daughter I used to have to wash the floors, and in those days you got on with it! And all the leather work in the smokeroom was studded, and you had to rub them down. And down the sides of the fireplace were brass stands at both sides, to cast the light up, and you had to make sure they were kept bright....and of course there wasn't carpets – it was all oilcloth. I had two cousins come and help at the weekend when we were so busy. There were about six of us working.*

Ron Powell: *You were expected to help in the business; my uncle, the eldest, he had to be up at six each morning to scrub the tile floors before he went to school. They used to have spittoons on the floor* (at the Bay Horse, Blossom Street). *These were made of vitreous iron, and they were kept on the floor near the passage bar, seldom in either of the rooms – but this is going back to 1926, that sort of time.*

10. Mr. and Mrs. Ron and Gladys Powell at the Bay Horse, Blossom Street. 1960s.

(Ron Powell)

People did cough a lot more in those days, there was a lot of T.B. about . . . and these spittoons were pretty much like a dog's feeding bowl, and they were filled with sawdust. They were used and then they were emptied and they were put in a bucket of disinfected water, and then the tap was left runnin'. I used to get the job of – I used to like the job – I was allowed to fill them with clean fresh sawdust and place them at strategic points around the counter.

Gill Thompson: *We had to sort out all the empty bottles into the correct crates every morning* (at the Edinboro Arms) *before we went to school, and it used to take us a good hour. On Sunday we had to take all the little miniatures down and clean them, novelty miniatures, loads of them . . . they all had to be cleaned, Sunday morning. There were wooden tables, we had to polish them all and polish the leather seatbacks and seats. We were expected to do a lot to help.*

Pauline Worthy: *When me dad died* (in 1951) *I took over doing the banking, then the books, I ran the pub* (the Talbot) *with my mother. When I met Norman* (her future husband) *in '54 I had to wait until the last customer had gone, when all the glasses and all the shelf filling were done, and only then was I allowed to go to a dance.*

Fred Veitch: *We all worked in the pub, you know. My eldest sister, the one that took the pub, she was a barmaid all the time. Sunday mornings we had to mop out, and all the brasses on the doors, they had to be polished. All the empty bottles had to be taken out, back into the bottle house, which I used to do on a Sat'day mornin'.*

22

11. The Veitch family (minus Fred) outside the Five Lions, Walmgate. 1940s. *(Fred Veitch)*

Doug Dalton: *After my father died, mother couldn't cope on her own. I was working at Craven's. I used to let the cleaner in in a morning, tidy all the bottles, jars and everything up, see the pumps were ready and go off to Craven's for 9 o'clock. My lunch hour was 12 'til 1.30. I used to run like hell to the Greyhound and I was behind the bar serving, trying to eat some lunch and then charge back for half past one. I used to leave Craven's at half past five, charge home, quick tea, and then most days I was behind the bar until 10 o'clock or half past. And it started to get to me a bit, so Peter* (his brother), *and Madge, who was the cleaner, used to come and help behind the bar.*

There were times when the customers rolled their sleeves up and gave a hand.

Pauline Coldrick: *They were nice people, warm hearted people* (at the Frog Hall). *If you were busy and needed another crate of beer from the cellar someone would go and get it for you, no question. They used to stay behind at night – obviously only a handful, three or four – and mop the bar floor, and then it would be fish and chips. Dad would pay for the fish and chips from Dai Prosser's and they'd stand and eat them and off they'd go home.*

Lela Norfolk: *You had to put a lot of hours in, but you didn't mind somehow, 'cos it wasn't like work, you were*

12. Horace Coldrick, and dog, behind the bar at the Frog Hall, Layerthorpe, around 1970. *(Pauline Coldrick)*

23

among friends. And if you were a bit stuck, somebody would bob down and help you. They all helped me out, 'specially when I was left on me own. They were right good.

Bob Barker: *They were very friendly to her* (the customers to his wife at the Brown Cow, when she was running the pub on her own). *The Romanies used to say, "We'll give you a hand", you know, Mary Mullen and Bernadette, and them.*

Sometimes the call of duty went beyond, what today would be considered acceptable limits.

Doreen Greaves: *On my wedding day I was scrubbing the front bar out* (at the Pack Horse) *while I was reading telegrams, congratulatory telegrams. Someone said, "Is somebody getting married here today?" I said, "Yes, me".*

13. Doreen Greaves relaxes with customers at the Lion and Lamb. c.1980. *(Doreen Greaves)*

Mabel Wilson: *I helped from eleven years of age,* (at the Edward V11) *I used to dry glasses. You were older in those days than you are now, you see. I had a very good home, but there was always something to do. When they washed the toilets out in the yard down the grates, you had to stone all round them. Jobs like that I had to do. At fourteen I used to look after the smokeroom, that was my job, I used to serve in there. There was a bell on each table and some on the walls, and I used* *to go through the bar to get the drinks. I missed out on my childhood because I've been working ever since.*

Of course the bigger more profitable pubs could employ staff – cleaners, barmaids, barmen.

Ron Powell: *When I was very young we used to have barmaids live in, they always came from the Durham area, Darlington, round there. Times were bad up there and girls were always pleased to get away from home, and they were paid approximately 10 shillings a week. They lived in and we gave them their food. We give them one day off a week, it wasn't Saturday or Sunday, it was, probably, whichever was the quietest day . . . and there was an unending supply. You put an advert in the 'Northern Echo' – and half a dozen applications arrived the next day. There was always a charwoman available, they used to come in for perhaps an hour and a half in the morning and swept the place right through. In the public bar there was a tiled floor; that was always scrubbed hands and knees – scrubbing brush and yellow soap. The old lady who scrubbed the floors, her name was Sarah Walker, she used to wear a sacking apron, hessian, like all charladies did. Yes, there was always someone to clean through. And they used to polish the brass with Brasso once a week perhaps, and on a different day – perhaps twice a week – the wooden arms of the benches would be polished, you could see your face in them.*

Joan Whitehead: *When we were really busy, summertime* (at the Spotted Cow), *there'd be eight or nine people working for us; barmaids, barman, waiter in the music room. In the early days you always had a waiter, same as at the Britannia. Give them a float and away they went.*

Barry Grayson: *We employed about twelve. We used to have six on, on a Saturday night; four staff, Marie and myself. Then of course it used to be five staff and Marie, with me on the door. We took some real money in those days, we really did.* (The late 1970s at the York Arms).

Doreen Bolton: *She* (her mother at the King's Head, Feasegate) *had two live-in barmaids, Deanna they called one, and Gertie. They used to be cleaners, then tarted up at night for t'barmaid's job.*

The accommodation for 'live-in' staff was often less than perfect:

Doreen Bolton: (Whilst working as a barmaid at the Black Swan, Coney Street). *There were two waitresses and two barmaids. And I remember the first night I stopped there – Lucy, the other barmaid, was leaning on t' bed, and I said, "What are you doin'?" She said, "Killin' bugs". Oh I nearly died!*

There were officials to deal with and book-keeping to do, but in earlier times business was carried out in a leisurely and gentlemanly fashion.

Pauline Worthy: *And in them days we never had a till. It was just a little wooden box that you pulled out, with divisions in it. And then all the ten bob notes, pound notes, fivers, they were all put under the black and white dogs* (ornaments) *and when my dad went to the races he just picked up the dogs, took a handful of notes. And that was the book-keeping system. Me dad did the book-keeping system, but how he made everything balance, I just don't know.*

Noel Attree: *Monday was the brewer's day. There was a feller called Bentley Waterhouse who worked for John Smith's, he was an elderly gentleman, very smart. He only seemed to wear grey checked suits, and carry a gladstone bag. And he used to come, and a little meal was prepared, and a drink. And all the drink you'd used was paid for, that was the brewer's bill, had to be ready on Monday.*

Mabel Wilson: *On Wednesday John Smith's came* (the brewer's rep.). *He used to come in a trap . . . he was a military sort with a bowler hat and a rather nice sports coat. And he had..well not a chauffeur..a man who drove the trap. When it was his day to come they all knew, 'cos there was drinks all round.*

Doug Dalton: *I used to have to go into Hunt's offices* (J.J. Hunt, the brewers) *with the order for beer, and I couldn't believe it, it was like going back to Pickwick's*

14. The Edward V11, Nunnery Lane. 1980.   *(Hugh Murray)*

days: these old gentlemen sitting scratching at these massive ledgers, these huge leather bound ledgers, placed on desks at 45 degrees, with a ledge. There was a row of these old gentlemen, never looked up, just scratching away in these ledgers – I assume it was just the accounting system. And I used to have to go with these hand-written orders for beer, hand it to one person, and it used to go down the line 'til it got to the end, and someone used to say, "O.K. it will be there".

By the 1970s the heavy hand of officialdom had descended on the tenant, and there were many people in authority to be dealt with.

Barry Grayson: *When he's the tenant, and it's his money, all the bills come down on his shoulders. You've got the V.A.T., you have the income tax – they don't believe anything you say . You've got the fire officer, the environmental health, particularly if you're doing food. You've got the brewery, who want to see results. You've got the police. And that's before you start; then you've got all the ramifications of the new legislation for people working – part-time staff have got to have the same rights as full-time staff – and you've got to have sick pay. If you're a tenant, you've got all these on your back.*

The main authority the licensee dealt with on a daily basis was the police force – the relationship between the police and the landlord has always been close. In Victorian times it was often stormy, as can be judged by an 1846 court case reported in the 'Yorkshire Gazette', where the licensee of the 'Cotherstone' in Hungate was alleged to have threatened to assault a policeman, 'with the soft end of this poker', for interrupting an impromptu prize fight that was taking place on the premises. The arrival of the twentieth century saw a more law abiding atmosphere prevail and a generally mutual respect came to exist between the two – particularly the beat constables. However this change was gradual, and there was friction between the police and some licensees into the 1920s, as these following extracts from L.V.A. committee meeting minutes confirm. November 1916: 'Two members reported on the rude and rough manner in which certain police officers spoke to licensed victuallers when visiting licensed premises'. June 1918: 'The Secretary reported that he had been in communication with the Chief Constable with reference to the insulting remarks made by Sergeant Williams of the City Police to Mrs. Stephenson of the Globe Inn on an occasion when he, on duty, visited the house at closing time'. But generally the regular visits of a police sergeant and a constable to licensed premises were very much welcomed by most publicans, who regret the day this practice stopped.

Barbara Fletcher: *Every Friday and Saturday night you would have the police sergeant with a constable, or a policewoman, and anybody under age would fly out. Now that was stopped, and it was the worst thing that ever happened in pubs. If policemen were still going round pubs, they wouldn't have all this hassle.*

G. FRENCH   J. PARKER   J. H. HORSFALL   A. B. HOLMES

R. FISHER   S. KIDDY   C. HERBERT   W. SMITH   F. HOGGARD   A. SLEIGHTHOLME   M. T. BOUSFIELD

| J. H. DARLEY | D. MOLLOY | A. E. GREAVES | C. GRAY | T. STEAD | J. H. ATHA | R. POWELL |
| *Secretary* | | *Senior Vice-President* | *President* | *Junior Vice-President* | *Hon. Treasurer* | *Past President* |

15. The Committee of the Licensed Victuallers' Association. 1960s.   *(David Atha)*

Doreen Greaves: *We liked the police to come in, if there was anything going on they used to calm things down. Between the wars* (at the Pack Horse) *when a policeman walked in, looking up and down the pub looking in the smokeroom and things, everybody used to behave themselves.*

John Greaves: *Yes, yes. In fact there was a period when they stopped the police visiting, and from a publican's view we didn't like that. We always got on well with the police – always.*

Pauline Coldrick: *I can remember in the early days* (at the Frog Hall) *when the uniformed policeman used to come round at odd times and see that everything was all right. And again, certain ones of those would go through to the back room and they'd have their pint of beer taken to them. Then, more latterly it was usually the C.I.D. who would come in, have a drink and a look round, and yes a very good relationship with them all the time.*

Joan Whitehead: *They* (policemen) *would be in the kitchen having a pint. We've sat, Norman and I, one o'clock in the morning, in the coffee room, knock on the window – copper, maybe two – made life more interesting.*

16. The Frog Hall, Layerthorpe. 1980. *(Hugh Murray)*

Pauline Worthy: *Police used to come in on a Saturday night* (at the Talbot Hotel), *uniformed coppers, and they'd walk through the pub, just walk through, say hullo to me dad. He'd pull two pints and go into the kitchen and they'd sit and talk. The detectives used to come in a lot and play dominoes with the customers, and I got to know them later on. I used to think how friendly they were, coming in and playing dominoes, but of course they were picking up bits of information and such like. I just thought they were nice people these policemen, they were nice, they used to bring me presents back from their holidays.*

Doreen Bolton: *Coppers used to come in after time, when they were on the beat* (at the Royal Oak), *and I always remember one night: Sergeant Ward and a copper came in, and they were in the door and they went to t' toilet and two Superintendents came in, who they were supposed to be reporting to. And I said to Wally* (her husband), *"Tell Wardy to stay where he is".*

Barry Grayson: *Always had a good rapport with the police, I was always on their side. If the police had to come to my place – I would only call them if I was really needing them – I was always prepared to help them in any shape, manner or form.*

However, relations with the higher echelons of the police force weren't always so friendly!

Noel Attree: *Inspector Williams was a great man in those days* (the 1920s). *He always used to emphasise that if ten o'clock was closing time, you asked for last orders at five minutes to ten. Ten o'clock, there shouldn't be a glass with any beer* *in it. You had five minutes to get out – and he meant it. He didn't come on his own, he always had two policemen with him. He was very, very strict.*

Joan Whitehead: *Inspector Iveson came in one Friday night* (at the Three Tuns which was then an ecclesiastical property and had to close one hour before other licensed premises). *My mother had just called 'time' at nine o'clock, and he looked at his watch and said, " Mrs Farrington, it's no good calling time if you don't enforce it, everybody should be out". It was about two minutes past nine!*

17. The Three Tuns, Coppergate. 1930s.   *(City of York Library)*

Too much drink could turn many a man who was decent when sober, into an obstreperous troublemaker. There were various ways of dealing with these customers, some physical, some psychological, some by sheer force of personality. Women could sometimes control troublemakers better than a man:

Noel Attree: *We had what we called the 'dram shop'. If you go in the Red Lion where the square in front of it is, you went in the right hand door, and this particular evening there were about three or four Irishmen in there goin' to have a right old punch up, they were gettin' very nasty. And my grandma walked into the bar, you know, looked over the counter, and she said to them, "What seems to be the trouble gentlemen?" And they looked at her – and this is honestly true – they said, "We're very sorry Mrs. Davison", and sat down, and there was no trouble. Can you imagine that happening today? If my grandma wasn't there and they fell out in the dram shop you had a job gettin' 'em out, you had to jump over the counter. What you did really was to turn 'em round fast. In those days Irishmen fought*

18. Landlady Christina Davison catches up with some paperwork on a sunny day at the Red Lion, Merchantgate. 1920s.   *(Noel Attree)*

with their fists in the air, and bring 'em fist down like they'd a hammer in their hands, and if they hit you, you went in the ground, but if you could turn 'em round and out, you were laughin' then! Yeah, but they were happy days.

Pauline Coldrick: *I remember one occasion* (in the Frog Hall) *having trouble with some Irish fellers who were going to fight, all I did, I banged on the bar – I knew I had plenty of back up with the local customers, they wouldn't have seen me* *struggle – but they went as meek and mild as anything. I just thumped on the thing and said, "Eh, stop that, drink your drink and get out" and they went as meek and mild as anything.*

Barbara Fletcher: *You had to be tough. I never had a bouncer on the door* (at the Londesbro' Hotel in the 1960s and 70s). *All these men had bouncers, I used to stand on the door on my own. I got some slagging off, but I managed it, I managed it. I never had any problems I couldn't cope with, I just used to say, "Sorry, but you're not getting served". I used to get called some cherished names. I used to get spit at, drum sticks thrown at me, and all sorts, when I wouldn't let a group in. It was a difficult life, but it was a good life.*

Doreen Greaves: *You got an odd patch* (in the Pack Horse) *where someone got excited, and my mother used to get stuck in. I remember once, there was a fight started and she went rushin' in to the bar and there was these great big Canadians, built like brick . . . you know, and she got stuck in like a terrier, "I'm*

not having this, I'm not having this", she was goin' . . . and one of them picked her up and put her on a table and said, "Oh shut up small fry". "Don't you small fry me!" (she said). *And they all set off laughin' and it passed over. Just passed over like that.*

Eve Briggs: *We had no riff-raff in, no way* (in the Bay Horse). *If a crowd of rough'uns came in I'd say "There's another pub up the hill, you won't be served in here". And I never had any bother.*

19. Marjorie ('Ma') Brown, landlady of the Pack Horse, Micklegate, from 1942 to 1955. *(Doreen Greaves)*

Of course most landlords preferred the 'softly, softly' and 'firm but fair' approach to trouble-makers:

Vera Lyall: *When the King William closed, a lot of them came over the road to us* (the Lord Nelson). *They were terrible, a lot of those. And Tony* (her husband) *was throwing some out, he used to just go and whisper something to them – this was any of them, as well as those that came from the 'William'. We got rid of them all eventually, I don't know where they went. He'd just turn and they'd say, "Right mister, all right mister". You never had any trouble with 'em and if you did he said, "Just sit there and have your drink. Don't make a noise". They were no trouble. If you went at them, they were trouble.*

Lily Grayson: *He once got his jumper torn* (her father at the Phoenix). *This chap called Neary, he was Irish, and he jumped over t'bar, and he actually tore the wool – but he just let it go. But once the same chap threw a glass of beer at me mother, she had one of these dresses on, it was made of marocain* (a kind of crepe), *and it crumpled it all up. He used to bar 'em and that was it. He never used to give in to let 'em back in. We used to have these two Harrison brothers used to come, and they used to fight like mad! One of 'em picked this marble clock off the mantelpiece, and he was going to throw it at me dad, anyway he barred 'em, but they kept coming back occasionally. He came in one night, did Tommy Harrison, and he was drunk, and he said, "I want a pint, and I'm not movin' 'til I get a pint". Me dad said, "Your not gettin' one, I'll shoot yer if you don't go" – he had a little sixpenny toy gun, you know, anybody could see what it was! So he said, "Tek me money", and threw it all over the bar.* Me dad said (to me), *"There you are, there's some pocket money to go to Scarborough with". Oh they were characters, them two.*

20. Lily Grayson (nee Gott) on right of picture. c.1938.   *(Lily Grayson)*

Eric Shaw: *There was one or two scuffles every now and then* (at the Angler's Arms) *. . . there were never any real punch-ups, even durin' the war. As I say me dad had a knack – I don't know how he did it, but he could talk 'em round, and that was that. I think he used to enjoy it actually, you know, he used to enjoy being able to do it.*

Pauline Coldrick: *My dad, he was a quiet sort of a man but he had a strong personality and he commanded a lot of respect really. And he wouldn't stand for any nonsense* (at the Frog Hall). *He would walk through occasionally, collecting glasses. He would have a word with them, he was fair with them, but yes, they respected him, and some were rough lads, one or two with slight bother with the police.*

John Greaves: *In our days the coaches used to use the yard* (at the Lion and Lamb) *as a park, and you can imagine maybe half a dozen buses, and they used to come staggerin' back from the races, you know, full of booze. And there used to be all sorts – well I use' to call 'em the tappers, tuckers and tatters. There was all the villains you could think of used to descend on us, there really was. There were a lot of problems, but you had to get round them the best way you could – you had to be a bit of a psychologist, you had to try and kid yourself to get rid of them.*

Sheila White: *But they never had bouncers on the door you know, never had bouncers like they do today. If a landlord said, "Out", they went. You really ruled t'place yourself. You didn't need bouncers. And if you told them no, you could bar them, and they wouldn't come over the step again.*

But the 'softly, softly' approach wasn't always applicable!

Vera Lyall: *He* (Tony) *had done P.T. courses in the army, he was athletic. There was one chap and he was in the bar* (at the Lord Nelson) *and he said something very rude to me, and Tony heard him and went round to him. This feller socked him one, so Tony hit him back and he fell on the floor in the bar. There wasn't anybody in, it was early on. I'm saying,"Oh I think you've killed him Tony". He said,"I'm sure I haven't". It was quite a while before he came to.*

Bob Barker: *Gadger, he was a shocker. He used to come in and say, "They call me the bull, I used to fight in the ring". And he used to turn awkward, he started once or twice. Second time I went round, he said, "I can make a mess of you". I said, "Oh can yer?" and picked up a chair and wrapped it round him. He reported me to t' police and they took me to court for taking the law into me own hands, and fined me £10. Yeah!*

Barry Grayson: *What I didn't realise was that there are a lot of homophobics in York* (the York Arms customers included members of the local 'gay' community) *and it didn't take me long to realise that we were the butt and target for these people; 'let's go and laugh at the queers' . . . I've heard so many things. I had my first fight on Christmas Eve 1976 through somebody doing this, and we chucked this most enormous feller out. York was getting very heavy, York was a nightmare on a Friday and Saturday night, there were phalanxes of drunken idiots coming up and down the street, and the snag is, once they got in, it was difficult to move them. And I decided to stand on the door, winter and summer, and I've stood on* *that door when I can't feel my hands or my feet – but the people inside were safely drinking. I must have barred hundreds, hundreds! I'm not a tough guy, but I won't back down. I've broke a couple of knuckles on people, I've certainly had a few bumps and bruises of my own. Then I got a bit long in the tooth, and I used to talk 'em out of it!*

A reputation as a 'tough guy' could help deter troublemakers:

Harry Atkins: *Sid* (Sid Staines, the landlord of the York Arms) *kept an orderly house. He was a big thick set feller . . . powerful feller, and you didn't argue with Sidney. He became known by people of that ilk who would come in with the express purpose of causing trouble, that it wasn't worth their bother 'cos Sid could deal with them.*

21. Sid and Kath Staines at the York Arms, Petergate. c.1970.   *(Harry Atkin)*

Edith Keech: *Bert* (her husband) *was a big man, he got to 25 stones, but when he was playing rugby he was seventeen* (stones). *There was never any trouble* (at the Minster Inn). *Bert saw to any trouble at the De Grey Rooms. He used to say, "Out, you're barred, I'm having no trouble in here". If it was early on, on a quiet night he would say, "Will you be all right, can you manage if I go next door to the club?"* (the Conservative Club). *Because he used to go playing snooker there, he was a good snooker player. He used to say, "Give me a ring if there's any trouble". But that was only occasionally.*

22. Bert Keech (with trade mark cigar) playing snooker at the Conservative Club, St. Leonard's Place. c.1950. *(Edith Keech)*

When things got really 'hairy', you could usually count on your regulars to 'get stuck in'.

Doreen Greaves: *We once had somebody cause trouble* (at the Lion and Lamb), *and there was only him* (John Greaves) *and me, and there were three of them, and we were going like the clappers of hell at the front of the pub. And all of a sudden a bus came down the street, and there was a squeal of brakes and a voice shouts, "I'm comin' John" and the bus driver pulled up. He left the bus in the middle of the street and came and helped us, so there was three of them against three of us, and they scarpered, and he got back on his bus and said, "Right John", and drove off.*

Vera Lyall: *There was one funny incident there* (the Three Cranes). *There was a chap in and Tony threw him out, and he went out and Tony followed him and this chap grabbed him by his tie, and he pulled his tie tight, and it was when they had the stalls down the side near where Gilbertson's shop* (the newsagents) *was, and they used to leave them there. And he's got Tony over this thing with his tie and Mick Stockhill – big lad Mick – he came out, 'cos he said, "Oh, Tony's being a bit of a long time, I better go and see", and he grabbed him and grabbed Tony off him and got his tie 'cos he was choking him* (Tony Lyall). *And he biffed him one,*

*and he went on this stall
and they left him there.
Shortly afterwards Mick
said, "I better go and see
if he's all right, like". Any
rate he'd gone. But there
were things like that. There
was always somebody in
there who you could rely
on.*

Lela Norfolk: *You could
get some right rough do's
if you weren't careful,
'specially when you were
there on your own. I
always had plenty of men
behind me, "cut that out",
that sort of thing.*

Problems with bad,
drunken behaviour on
licensed premises were, in
the era covered by this
book, generally of an
individual and isolated
nature, but not always so,
as the following extract

23. Vera and Tony Lyall at the Three Cranes, St. Sampsons
Square. 1970s.   *(Vera Lyall)*

from the minutes of an L.V.A. committee meeting held in January 1923 confirms:
'With regard to the case of disorderly conduct and assault at the King's Arms Hotel,
Fossgate, the Secretary was directed to see the Chief Constable, to impress upon
him the opinion of the committee that Small (the defendant) should be severely dealt
with, as he was one of an organised gang who caused terror to the womenfolk in
hotels and pubs. That up to the present he has managed to evade the full penalty of
the law, and that it was suggested that Small ought to be ordered to leave town.' (!)
(Later the same month the Yorkshire Evening Press reported the court case, in which
the defendant was accused of using filthy language, throwing beer over the landlady
and spitting in her face. Small was found guilty of being disorderly, but not guilty
of assault. Despite having 37 previous convictions, including assaults on the police
and unlawful wounding, he was only fined £1 and bound over for 12 months.)

Even in the 1950s there were groups of men whose presence on licensed premises
was feared:

Betty Harris: *There was a family . . . and they were rugby players. Now they were the nearest you got to crime in York. The grapevine would go round, "They're out", this would be Saturday night. It would be a huge big deal if they came in.*

'Time off' was often spent in the company of fellow publicans. The Licensed Victualler's Association – the publicans' 'trade union' – organised many outings, dinners and dances. The York branch of the L.V.A. is one of the oldest in the country, being formed in 1845 and holding its first annual dinner in the De Grey Rooms in 1848, when around one hundred publicans attended. The formal dinner-dances were looked forward to with anticipation, giving opportunity to landladies to flaunt their finery. They also liked to look their best for the more mundane committee meetings.

Pauline Worthy: *And then you had your committee meeting that you hosted at your pub, and all the ladies'd come round. And that was a big occasion when they came to your pub, and you had to put on the afternoon tea, and all the best crockery came out, and you all got dolled up in your best finery and jewellery.*

Gill Thompson: *If my parents were going to licensed victuallers' do's, they'd look so wonderfully handsome. My dad used to be the Senior Vice President, my mum got to be President of the Ladies' Auxiliary. It was always a really formal ball. We loved to see them because they looked so absolutely wonderful. She looked like a princess when she was all dolled up for these balls and banquets.*

24. Nellie and Harry Atha at the Bay Horse, Monkgate, shortly before their retirement. Mr. and Mrs. Atha and their son David, who took over the reins at the Bay Horse from his parents, were active members of the L.V.A. for many years.
(David Atha)

Eric Shaw: *They were both tied up in various sections of t'Licensed Victualler's* (his parents at the Angler's Arms). *All*

38

*the ladies – as I had to call
'em – they used to like getting
dressed up in their finery . . .
she* (his mother) *loved her fur
coat. All these ladies, they all
did the same thing – big hats,
fur coats. 'Course when they
went out together, they looked
like duchesses.*

Lela Norfolk: *We would see
who could outdo the other. It
suited me, I liked it! We did
used to think we were
somebody. Even in them days,
all those years ago* (the late
50s, early 60s) *they had some
lovely clothes you know. I had
an ermine cape – I suppose I
thought that was fancy.*

Lily Grayson: *They used to
go to these balls at the De
Grey Rooms, you know, get all
dressed up. I used to love to
see me mum dressed up in her
long dress, and me dad with*

25. The Mount Hotel landlady, Lela Norfolk, and escort, at an L.V.A. function. 1960s.   *(Lela Norfolk)*

*t'pussy bow on. When they came home me mum used to say, "I'm not going with
him anymore, he was beating time with a lump of celery".*

The L.V.A. also organised trips out, and not just local ones.

Eric Shaw: *Me dad'd maybe go with the Licensed Victualler's, with Mr
Fieldhouse and Mr Gill from Church Street, they were all on the committee. They
used to say it was a conference, they'd maybe go away for four days or summat
like that, to Blackpool. Me mother would do t' same with the women's section.*

Sheila White: *I've been all over with them, Scotland, go to distilleries. You'd get
invitations to go to all the distilleries, and the wineries down in London. We went
over to Ireland to Guinness, to Cork.*

Nights out at the theatre were also enjoyed. Complimentary tickets to the 'Empire'
in Clifford Street or the Theatre Royal were often available.

Noel Attree: *In those days a theatrical bill was put up in there* (the Red Lion),
*and for that you got two free tickets. Me grandma used to go every Monday in Bob
Whitehead's taxi . . . a Dodge.*

26. L.V.A. committee members on a visit to the Ind Coope Brewery on the 11th September 1952. The group includes well known York licensees: Messrs Gofton, Powell, Atha, Shaw and Mrs. Hardy. *(David Atha)*

Doreen Bolton: *You advertised what was comin' on the 'Empire', and you used to get a free pass. It was called 'landladies' night out'. We all used to go – old Mrs. Wright who had the 'Fox', Annie Hardy, Annie Nelson, Meg Cross, Lil Shaw that had the 'Anglers'. It was great. I remember once comin' home and talkin' to Wally and I put my arm on the counter, you know, and I fetched all the trays off. "Come on, you've had enough". I said, "I know I 'ave, but we've had a good laugh", and we did, we did.*

Ron Powell: *The Theatre Royal used to put bills through the door, and you could have two seats, dress circle or stalls, every week, and about every six weeks you got a pass for two at the Leeds Grand Theatre. Always Bertram Mills Circus, two free passes – very good seats as well – circus people were always generous.*

Mabel Wilson: *We got free tickets for the 'Empire', I went with me mother. There was a little shop in Petergate – Moorhouses, and they used to make little meat pies with lovely gravy, they were about two for fourpence or something. We used to have these as a treat when we came out of the first house at the 'Empire'.*

Doreen Greaves: *Me father used to take us to the 'Empire' every Tuesday* (from the Pack Horse). *And I used to wash all the glasses that were left over from lunch-time and tidy round the bar – and I found out afterwards that he'd a free pass!*

27. The Ladies' section of the L.V.A. at the Guinness Brewery. 1960s.   *(Lela Norfolk)*

Landlords enjoyed the company of their peers during their free time.

Ron Powell: *There was what was known as the '25 Club', which met in the Elephant and Castle in Skeldergate. It may have been formed in 1925 or been restricted to twenty five members; George Hopwood from the Coach and Horses in Nessgate, Frankie Beckett – he used to have the Elephant and Castle – Joe Shacklock from the 'Mount', he would be a member. They were, really, bit of the lads, the whole lot of them, they used to play pranks on one another. They used to have a concert artiste, usually a comic, perhaps a tenor.*

Noel Attree: *Publicans, they'd have a night out together. I know my Uncle John (John Davison from the Red Lion), I've gone with him when I got to eighteen. They'd always call at the Blue Bell in Fossgate to see old Mr. and Mrs. Robinson, they were alive then. And it was always a good little pub, warm, comfortable, good company, good pint of beer.*

Pauline Worthy: *I remember there was always somebody held back. Annie Melson, she used to have the Three Cranes, me dad would always walk her home. And Mrs. Wright who had the Fox in Petergate, she was another landlady on her own, so he would walk her home. They all stuck together, very rare we had any outside friends.*

Doreen Bolton: *Mrs Cross* (a fellow landlady) *and me mother used to get tarted up to t'nines when it was Armistice Day, then do all the pubs. Real day out for 'em it was, and it was supposed to be a sad day – queer goin' on!*

28. The Three Cranes, St. Sampson's Square. 1950s.   *(City of York Archives)*

Publicans were often too fond of their own product.

Sheila White: *I never had a drink during the day, I used to drink lime and lemon, I wasn't a drinker. You see a lot of them get on the bottle, oh yes, it's fatal. You'd get a drunken landlord or a drunken landlady.*

Doreen Bolton: *Me old dad, bless 'im, he did like drink you know, and he used to go to t'turkish bath in t'market to get the booze soaked out of 'im. And me mother used to say, "Go and see if your father's in t'turkish bath". Well that feller in t'turkish bath, he'd lily white legs and he used to have a dressin' gown on and a big ear trumpet and I used to say, "IS ME DAD IN"? He'd say, "Yes". I'd say, "TELL 'IM I'M HERE". Me dad used to come out and I'd say, "Me mam sent me for yer, yer goin' to cop it". I used to walk him home, bless him, and I was always frightened he would fall. He used to creep up stairs and I always used to stand at t'back of 'im, cos I was frightened he would fall – he'd have knocked me arse over tip if he'd fell! And me mother would say, "Was he in"? I said, "No, I bet he's in bed mam, having a lie down".*

29. Austin Gretton stands in the doorway of his pub, the King's Head Hotel, Feasegate. 1922.

(Doreen Bolton)

Many landlords and landladies enjoyed socialising with their customers, on trips or 'at home'.

Vera Lyall: *We used to play in the Pickering league* (the dart team at the Three Cranes). *And we used to have teams go out there as far as Scarborough and Filey and various places, and we used to have lovely times. Your life was all around your pub, didn't have any other life at all.*

Pauline Worthy: *On a Sunday mornin' me dad would have all the pints lined up on the bar, ready for opening the doors, 'cos all the men would be standing on the corner of the street, waiting for opening times. And they'd come in, and it was a panic, "For you Fred, and yours are two milds" – he knew everybody's drink. Domino boards would be set up, just for him to go and sit down and start playing the dominoes on a Sunday morning.*

2. FAMILY LIFE

Bringing up a family in a pub had both good and bad sides. Good, when the mother could combine domestic and business duties under the same roof, and having a regular income meant there was always food on the table – indeed many publicans were very well off compared to the majority of their customers, and considered themselves 'in business'. On the down side, mother and father were usually working long hours and the children were often left to their own devices. Family life for the licensee often included extended families. There was a tradition for dynasties to be developed – it was not unknown for multiple numbers of pubs to be run from within one family group.

The children of publicans often felt denied a proper family life, feeling 'on view' or 'left out' or alternatively being expected to 'pull their weight'. This usually brought a reaction in later life, when the thought of being 'in the business' was either loved or hated.

Eric Shaw: *We were never brought up in a family environment. Other kids, they'd maybe sit at home playing cards or dominoes with their parents, things like that, but that never happened to me. They had to be open at half past five and didn't call time 'til half ten. I never took to a pub, I never liked it. I don't drink now and I won't go in a pub . . . I feel uneasy . . . I'm not at home.*

Pauline Coldrick: *I was about twenty four when my mother died and I said, "Right, I'll give up work and help you with the pub". And he knew* (her father) *that I hated it anyway, I resented the pub deeply by the time I got to teenage. And he said, "No you won't, you've got your life to lead, stay where you are".*

Ron Powell: *As children my sister and I were neglected, my mother and father were in business, we weren't supervised. When it was obvious that my mother and father were going to have to retire shortly, all the customers said, "Are you going to take it on Ron?" and I said, "No way, I didn't enjoy my childhood here – I've helped out when I've done a day's work and hadn't really wanted to do". It wasn't for me.*

Doreen Bolton: *You see when you're in a pub, you have a funny childhood. I mean I never, ever, remember me mother comin' up to read a bedtime story. Me dad did, but never me mother.*

Fred Veitch: *It's not a good family life . . . it's not a life for children, it isn't a place to bring children up in. I don't say that we suffered for it, maybe we had a better standard of living, and that counteracted the fact that you didn't see much of your parents. If I'd have had a lad I'd mebbe liked to take 'im to rugby or football. He* (his father) *didn't have time to be involved, he could never take you fishin' or anything like that.*

Pauline Worthy: *No, it wasn't happy being in a pub, you never saw your parents . . . they'd come and say, "Aren't you ready for bed yet?" Once or twice my mother would put me to bed, but I was detached, they ran the bar, it was a busy pub, and that was number one. And you weren't allowed to make a noise on an afternoon because my parents wanted to sleep, so we played outside. I was taken out for meals, and I was well dressed and well shod, but I never went round town with my dad, never went anywhere with both parents. And that's how it was. The pub always came first.*

Van Wilson: *I was about four, and at lunchtime they used to sit me on the bar and various customers would chat to me and make a fuss of me. They must have trained me to say it, but when someone asked, "What will you have?" I used to say, "A gin and orange please". This was lemonade and orange juice. I must have been a sort of mascot, to add a bit of colour. But then my mother was quite ill and had to spend time in hospital. I had a great-aunt who lived with my grandparents and she sometimes looked after me. My grandparents were in one pub (the White Swan, Goodramgate) and my parents were in another pub (the Britannia, Nunnery Lane) and so my mum was a vague figure to me at that time. She seemed to be either ill in bed or working. It wasn't a happy time. She didn't participate a lot in the running of the pub and I think she just wanted to get out, and so they left the trade and our life changed.*

30. Moira and Geoff Potter enjoy a drink with two R.A.F. friends at the Britannia, Nunnery Lane. Late 1950s. *(Van Wilson)*

Then there was the alternative view:

Sheila White: *Oh my family life with my children? They did very well because they were never left out. Patrice* (her daughter) *was five when we went into licensed premises. David* (her son) *was thirteen. By the time he was eighteen he could run the bars for us. Patrice didn't lose out and everyone in the pub loved her. When it was her birthday and Christmas they used to bring her presents in. And she looked after the pub when she got older, when we were at the 'Ox'* (the Castle Howard Ox). *They had a good time, they enjoyed it.*

31.   Jim and Sheila White at the Castle Howard Ox, Townend Street. 1970s.   *(Sheila White)*

Joan Whitehead: *My mother used to say, "Come and give me a hand" and I said, "Oh no, I'm not working in a pub". And eventually she said, "I want some help tonight, I haven't a barmaid. Just come and wash the glasses for me, you'll be all right". And I was washing the glasses when my mother said, "There's someone to see you, Joan". It was my aunt and she said, "Two bottles of Magnet, and I want Joan to serve me". I was petrified really. Anyway I did it and a gentleman standing next to Auntie Jean said, "I'll have a pint Joan, while you're there". Panic again! Then I thought, "This isn't so bad after all". And I spent the rest of my life in the business.*

Judy Plaxton: *I was always involved* (as a teenager at the Nag's Head). *I wanted to get in there and do something, you know, like washing up. When I got older I used to go and serve in the bar, you know. I loved it.*

Publicans could make a good living, their families rarely went short of food or clothing. Holidays away were common, and their children were sometimes privately educated. Many publicans were considered 'well to do', certainly if they were tenants – rather than managers – as most pre-war publicans were. The gap in status between the landlord and his customers, in some pubs, can be judged by the following extracts from the minutes of an L.V.A. meeting held in May 1943:

'Arrangements for the golf match were made. The executive would very much appreciate any assistance with the refreshments . . . as there were many licensees whose customers would not have any interest in golf, it would be better to leave each individual licensee to do what he liked as regard to this'. (!)

Eve Briggs: *We used to go on three or four holidays a year, wonderful, always first class holidays. We used to go on cruises.*

Doreen Bolton: *Me dad used to play dominoes when we had the King's Head, and go to the 'Starre' and play for a fiver a time – which was a lot of money wasn't it?* (around 1925). *We had a nanny when Joe* (her brother) *was born, and we took Nanny to Blackpol with us – she always used to stop in t'best hotel did me mam, nurse maid and all. Emma* (her grandmother, Emma Gretton) *was a real character. She had two licences at once did me granny; where t'barracks is at Fulford* (formerly the Barrack Tavern), *she had the Talbot in Church Street. Austin and Maud* (two of Emma Gretton's children) *were educated in France – Dijon. She owned most of Orchard Street at one time, then she had some houses near . . . was it Swann Street?*

Eric Shaw: *I never wanted for owt, I always had a push bike and say roller skates. I allus had toys, I had a beautiful electric train set at one time. Shall we say the average lad I went to school with never had owt like that.*

Mabel Wilson: *We had a car, it was like a charabanc* (around 1918 at the Edward V11). *We would never go out with him* (her father) *because he was so proper – he would stop at Nessgate and he'd have to get out to wind it up again. But he'd let us have it if we had someone to take us for a drive, we could go to Scarborough for the day. It was just like 'Chitty Chitty Bang Bang', it was a Wolseley, real old fashioned one, and we had that for a long time. My mother was very strict, I got a good slapping for going to the Salvation Army dinner one day. She said, "That wasn't for you, you get plenty at home".*

Ron Powell: *My mother and father were able to do things they never would have if my father had been following his own job, with a terraced house to live in. We were always well dressed – I don't say that my mother had great pretensions, but she wanted to appear to have done the right thing. I went to Scarcroft School when I was five you see, and she used to come down to school with a jug and a cup. And in the cup was ovaltine, made with milk, and a cloth placed over it to keep it warm. It was handed through the school railings. We used to take a holiday until me grandmother died in . . . was it 1937? We used to take our holidays together, me mother and father and us two* (Ron and his sister) *in a Blackpool boarding house for a week.*

Noel Attree: *There was one lad who played with me, me grandma said to him one day, "Stop and have a bit of dinner", and me grandma had done steak and kidney,*

32. The Powell family from the Bay Horse, Blossom Street and the Claytons from the Wheatsheaf, Nunnery Lane, on a day out together at Filey around 1935. Mrs. Powell senior is sitting with a blanket across her knees. Mrs. Clayton is sat on her left. *(Ron Powell)*

33. The off-licence shop in Swann Street, which was run by Sheila White's grandparents, George and Elizabeth Newland, and where Mrs. White was born. 1930s.

with a Yorkshire puddin'. It was always nice you know. Nellie or Ada Sherwood, who ever was there – two sisters – would cook it and see to it, grandma would just see that it was all right. And this kid was in tears, he says, "I never eat meat". This lad had never eaten meat, and that's true.

Pauline Worthy: *We always had somebody in to do the cooking, and I think they made the beds too, like housekeepers. My mother never did it, they were too busy. I never learned to cook, because when I came home from school a meal was put in front of me. I couldn't have certain people back at the pub because they were working class. I didn't go out and get one pair of shoes, me dad bought me two pairs. And that was the kind of difference livin' in a pub, you were that little bit well off.*

Barry Grayson: *Before V.A.T. came in I must say, if you ran a good pub, you had a licence to print money.*

Even running a busy 'off-licence' could provide a decent living.

Sheila White: *Our off-licence* (in Swann Street in the 1920s and 30s) *was a full off-licence, selling spirits, bottled and draught beers, and we sold as much in our*

*off-licence as people sold in
public houses. We had an old
scrubbed table in the scullery
and there were pint jugs with
people's initials on. Me
grandmother used to leave
the back scullery door open,
put the beer in before she
went to bed. When she got up
in the morning the beer had
gone and the money would
be in the jug. The men, when
they were on night duty, they
came in, and they always
paid. I used to have my coats
tailor- made at Mr. Frost's on
Ouse Bridge, and I used to
have my shoes made at
Poole's in Micklegate. I had
a better life then than I have
now.*

There was a great family
tradition in the pub trade. One
late nineteenth century York
landlord and his wife, Joe and
Elizabeth Pritchard, had nine
children, seven of whom
became publicans. They had
more than ten grandchildren
who were publicans, or

34. The Market Tavern, Coppergate, in 1910. The shirt
sleeved figure on the right of the picture is the landlord,
Thomas Stainthorpe. The pub was later tenanted by Alf
Lock, a New Zealander, and his wife Ethel, an aunt of
Noel Attree. *(John Terry)*

married to publicans. Between them all they were the licensees of more than thirty
different York public houses. Doreen Bolton and Tony Lyall were, and Doreen
Greaves and Noel Attree are, members of this family.

Doreen Bolton: *I think we must have owned more pubs in York than anybody.
There was Eddie, Arthur, Austin* (her uncles) *and me grandma, they all had pubs
at the same time.*

Sheila White: *Me Aunt Maria, she had Shaw's Hotel in Trinity Lane, me Aunt Ada
had the Trafalgar. My dad's Aunt, Mrs. Parker, she had Parker's Hotel – you
know, Stubbs – well that was hers. They had a snooker room upstairs and a dance
hall – that was when I was a child. Several aunts and cousins had hotels and pubs
in York.*

3. THE PREMISES

During the second half of this century many changes have taken place in the fixtures and fittings and general lay-out of both public and private rooms of York public houses. Many previously small-roomed, ill-furnished premises have changed dramatically and out of recognition. In many cases the changes were for the good and licensed premises became more welcoming to the more varied clientele they were seeking to attract. However there were also alterations that destroyed the character of many inns – centralised design by the breweries producing houses that are homogenised, bland and lacking in distinction. In this chapter, publicans and family members describe the pubs they inhabited, telling us of both the public and private areas in which they lived and worked.

Some breweries treated their premises as purely places to sell ale and paid little attention to the comfort of the customer or the manager or tenant – although the private accommodaton was usually (but not always!) of a far higher standard than that of the pubs' customers.

Judy Plaxton: *They used to say you can sell John Smith's beer in a shed. They never bothered about the decor . . . it desperately needed seeing to* (the Nag's Head, Heworth in the 1950s). *It was the beer people went for.*

35. The Nag's Head, Heworth. 1950s. *(City of York Archives)*

Bob Barker: *They said there was a pub going, was we interested?* (The Sam Smith's brewery, speaking of the Brown Cow). *My wife wasn't interested, she said, "It's filthy", which it was at the time. Anyway, we took it, and we cleaned it up. For about six or seven weeks we never saw a customer, 'cos it was runnin' wick in mice . . . oh! We had to get them in* (rodent controllers). *Upstairs there was a built-in wardrobe in one of the bedrooms. Well it was screwed down and when I opened it, it was full of hen feathers, they must have been pluckin' 'em upstairs! Shockin'! We had to have it all done out.*

Eric Shaw: *He was always a tenant* (his father at the Angler's Arms in the 1930s), *and from that point of view you could never get anything done by John Smith's. John Smith's just did not want to improve it, quite honestly. The living conditions were terrible. We had one room, which we called the kitchen – ground floor, back of the pub. There was an old pot sink, just cold water, we'd be looking out from the sink into the yard, and all t' men who went to t' urinal passed the window. There'd be no toilet for t' men, just the urinal.*

36. The Brown Cow, before its redevelopment. 1920s.
(The City of York Archives)

There was a flush toilet a bit further down the yard, but that was for the ladies, the women. Our livin' conditions were in this square room, it was very high, I would have thought that at sometime it was one room above another, as if the floor had been taken out. There was a door leading into a similar sort of place at t' side, which we called t' back kitchen, and that was of t' same height. Me mother had a gas cooker in there, she had to cook in there – it was little more than a shed really – and then come into the other room. We kept bikes in there . . . and me mother had an old cast iron mangle with wooden rollers on, she did the washing in there. We had no bathroom, what we had was a little tin bath, and all the water was boiled up in an old copper kettle . . . and filled by buckets. We were bathed Friday night, and when we'd got rid of all the customers me dad and me would lift the bath, one at either end, and just tip it down the yard, in other words we washed the yard out on Friday night. It really was terrible livin' conditions. The floor of the kitchen, it was uneven, it was virtually an earth floor. She did what she could, she tried (his mother) they battled against it . . . there were mice all over t' place, it was riddled with mice, me dad would set traps night after night. Blackclocks weren't swarming all over, but you did see 'em, you either stood on it quick or hit it with a shovel. Oh it was basic.

37. The Angler's Arms, Goodramgate. *(The City of York Archives)*

Ron Powell: *The living areas in those days* (at the Bay Horse) *were not unlike the living areas of the most modest of houses, it was primitive in the twenties and thirties. No one would live in places like that these days.*

38. The Talbot Hotel, Church Street. 1950s.   *(Pauline Worthy)*

Pauline Worthy: *It wasn't plush* (at the Talbot). *Leatherette seats, a seat with a back rest, all the rooms were like that. And big, heavy metal tables, with Britannia on the legs of them and a little thing on the bottom to stand your drinks on, and a grid, and a wooden top. Bar stools . . . it wasn't plush, it wasn't comfy, there was no dralon in them days. It was all working men, wash it down and keep it clean, type of thing. It was all painted . . . over thick paper. I mean the ceiling and walls were all nicotine and brown, and once a year you would probably wash them all down. You didn't spend a lot then. I remember in the bar room when linoleum squares came in, where you put adhesive down and stuck the squares on. That was very exciting in our pub, when we had those put down, we were kind of leaders. Me dad was very excited then!*

Doug Dalton: *It would be late '56 when we moved into this sumptuous palace!* (The Greyhound, Spurriergate). *I don't honestly think they'd had a good look round, because mother was quite upset at first. The tale father told us, was that the previous landlord had not lived on the premises for many years. The problem of getting furniture alone upstairs – it was a beautiful, circular, wrought iron staircase – was horrendous. Whitby Oliver's moved us, and everything had to be literally carried over their heads and round the corners, upstairs. And there wasn't a floor in the Greyhound that was level. Beds, everything, had to be propped up on books or wood to get things level. I've never forgotten the main passage, which went the full length, it was at an angle of 45 degrees, and there were four or five layers of lino on this floor – they started to take some up, but gave it up as a bad job. The bathroom? That was straight out of Victorian days. The bath was very large, chipped enamel, with the biggest brass taps I'd ever seen, with the most revolting shower attachment. We never used it, because a long time after we moved in the water ran brown, what came out of the taps was a bit like Worcester Sauce. My mother used to have to go and get buckets of clean water from the pork butchers, which was slightly down from the pub. The kitchen was quite a size, it had a very, very, large Victorian range. When we got a cleaner she used to black lead this thing and it used to shine. There was a gas stove in, I've never forgotten that, because the last time I'd seen one like it was during the war.*

Downstairs was one very long bar, they said in those days it was one of the longest bars in York, it just went on into the distance and slightly curved round the corner. There was a snug in the front, and in it was a very beautiful wrought iron table. The snug was so small that you get four people – maybe five at a pinch – and that was it, it was full. The old Victorian stove was one of these large, pot-bellied efforts, and it used to be stocked up with coke, and this was in the bar. And it wasn't attached to the wall, it was almost in the middle of the floor, and when it got hot, it used to glow red with the heat from it. If you'd touched it, you'd have been badly burned. It was unbelievable the heat that came from it, I was always amazed it never caused a fire. When they knocked the Picture House (cinema) *down to extend Woolworth's, we got absolutely over-run with mice. And for some reason when the boiler, as we called it, was cooling down, these mice used to go under it, and when the cleaner came in in a morning she used to clean the boiler, set fire to it. And when it was glowing these mice used to come staggering out – unbelievable. You could have kicked them, swatted them. We had two cats at the time. Those poor cats, it got to the point where they'd had enough. They just used to take no notice of these mice. Occasionally they'd eat one, if they got a bit peckish. And that went after they built the new Woolworth's, but there was nothing you could do about it. You could put a trap down, you could trap twenty a day, it didn't make the slightest difference. I didn't know mice could climb, until I saw them going up the wall, they'd be in the bedrooms, they'd be everywhere.*

39. The Greyhound Hotel, Spurriergate. 1950s.
(Patricia Hall)

Mabel Wilson: *It was quite nice* (at the Edward V11). *We had four bedrooms . . . a bath room with the bath in the middle of the room, not boarded in like they are now. We had a private loo; the toilet was the best part of it, because it was a press flush like they are now – no chain, press – and it was inside, it was separate from the bathroom, which was marvellous really. But the accommodation was really very good.*

Doreen Bolton: *It was a nice little pub* (the King's Head). *There was a kitchen downstairs, and we had a tin bath, and I had to stand on t'door so nobody would come in while me mother was having a bath, 'cos kitchen was on t'level with t'bar and t'smoke-room. And there was a big copper in there and they used to get blackclocks in it. And me mother bought a thing where you put jam on it, and they walked on it and got tipped in to the bottom, and me brother, our Jack, and*

56

Georgie Douglass, another publican's son, used to empty this thing on my head! We had seven rooms to kip in, and there was a dining room and a big sitting room – it went all across the front – and another little room we used to play in.

Noel Attree: *In the parlour* (at the Red Lion), *you opened the door and there was a writing desk under the window that overlooked the square. Nice carpet, big, red carpet. A nice table, beautiful table, polished ... shaped, but not oval. On the left was an old fashioned rosewood piano. Then there was a nice settee..there were one or two nice pictures, but I can't remember those. There was a big lovely sideboard, beautifully furnished with all sorts of dishes and vases, and there were two nice chairs, no arm rests, a back and a seat. There was a very*

40. The Red Lion, Merchantgate. 1930s.
(City of York Library)

nice fireplace in there, sort of blue with gold lines on. And on the mantelpiece she had a matching clock, and two ornaments on either side. There was a door papered over (with the same paper that was in the room) *and you could go through to a room on the other side, that was grandma's bedroom.*

Barry Grayson: *Those two lounges* (at the York Arms) *were two separate rooms at one time, they had doors on them until '61. And the carpet came from the Q.E.2. It was bought from Whitby Oliver's, and it was like the end of the roll. It was done in '66, it cost . . . I think it was £9 a square yard. It lasted fourteen years, I think the pile must have been threequarters of an inch thick. And they made the carpet and brought it, stitched and cut, and rolled it out, and it fitted! And a story Kath* (the previous landlady) *was telling everybody – that there's this guy stood with a pint, and he put his fag down and did that to it* (indicating it being stubbed out on the floor). *It's a brand new carpet! It's only been laid five minutes beforehand! Kath pointed out the errors of his ways!*

Some premises were old, with creaking floorboards, dark rooms, and long, and not always happy, histories. No wonder then, that things 'went bump in the night'.

Harry Atkins: *Myself and me mother and father stayed temporarily at the York Arms to assist my sister, and I was sleeping in the back bedroom upstairs, along with me father. And I woke up in the early hours of the morning, and I was aware of a sensation, a rather cold feeling in the bedroom. And I observed something that looked to me similar to a beehive, and it wasn't as tangible as a teatowel fluttering about, but it was more tangible than mist. Eventually me dad woke up and I drew his attention to it, and he said he could see the same thing and we were both a bit scared. It seemed to be floating above the ground at the base of one of the wardrobes. It only lasted, from memory, a few minutes. I've never seen anything since that day, but my sister used to maintain that they had a clothes brush upstairs that was backed with brass, and occasionally this clothes brush would be reversed, but I never witnessed anything like that, I never witnessed anything from October 1958.*

Eric Shaw: *We* (his sister and himself at the Angler's Arms) *were on the second floor, there were just these two rooms, oh it was weird, old wooden stairs, floorboards creaked. I remember my bedroom, the floors sloped, it was all sloped down, like these old buildings you see where all the doors are sloping and the door jambs don't fit – it was cold air, no central heating, no hot water. It was just a case of getting under t'blankets with the hot water bottle – it really was terrible.*

41. Mrs. Lilian Shaw unconvincingly pulls a pint at the Anglers Arms. 1940s. *(Eric Shaw)*

The old gas lamps were still on the wall upstairs on the landin', and the taps were still there. There was a sitting room upstairs, which was never used. It was done out in a three-piece suite and sideboard – we never went up there. All this talk about ghosts – I'm convinced I saw one once in the Angler's Arms. I went to bed one night and it was dark. For some reason I woke up, I don't know why, I woke up – and I looked down from my bed, and there was definitely a grey shape in that room, there was something in that bedroom. It never did anything, it didn't upset me, it never made a noise or something like that. I wasn't frightened, but I can see it now. I'm convinced there was a ghost in the place.

Bob Barker: *Going back a number of years, the ghost. Some of the old people remember him. She'd run off with somebody else, and he'd got drunk or something, and he was carrying a case down* (into the cellar) *'cos they were steep, but there was like a corner step, you see. It started narrow and came out, and was almost covering the next step, and he missed and went straight down and broke his neck. They found him dead afterwards, they wondered why he hadn't opened up. They got in, and found him down there. I never saw it, no not me, but my wife had seen it twice, she'd just seen the face* (in the cellar). *She said it wasn't cruel, it was whiskered, you know, big sidechats, and she said that's all it was. The dog wouldn't go* (down into the cellar). *I used to say, "Come on", but no, he wouldn't. I carried him down once, you know, I thought I'll just take him down, and whoosh!! Straight upstairs and off!! Josh Davies the landlord before me, he'd seen it, so it must be right.*

Barry Grayson: *We had a very heavy stool, which the legs came out slightly. Four legs, sturdy, really heavy stool, made of solid wood, seat about two inches thick. And one night Marie's in the bigger of the two bars at the back, and I'm at the doorway into the bar, by a table, next to the hat rack. And there's such a bloody crash, and this thing's fallen over on its side. How on earth did it fall over? We used to say: "She's at it again". If we said anything, we said, "Look, this has happened, we are not making anything up, and you must judge whether you believe it or not".*

Although many pubs did not meet the 'comfort standard' demanded today, they were individual places which had developed over decades and had character and 'personality' which only age and respectful treatment could bring about. There was also the fact that in an age before the 'throw away society' when resources were short, changes to decor, furnishings and general refurbishment were kept to a minimum, and 'make do and mend' was the order of the day.

Ron Powell: *The seating consisted of settles all the way round, continuous seating round the room and covered in leather cloth, a lot of it a very shiny finish, and that was always polished up and kept very bright indeed. The arms where it came to an end were made of mahogany, and they were polished, you could see your*

*face in them. Every table in the place had a bell on it, the type where you struck a
knob on the top, and it gave a single note. They were always polished to a high
degree, very bright indeed. And these bells all had slightly different notes. I don't
know if this was intentional, but they ranged from a fairly high 'ping' to a very
sonorous 'sheep gong' type of note. And when you heard that noise from the back
of the bar you knew which table to go to. If the sheep gong sounded – sometimes
twice to denote urgency! – that meant Mr. Wright was ready for another drink.
And so we knew to go for a whisky, with an equal amount of lemonade on top of it,
and change in your hand for a shilling in case it was needed.*

*Pubs are done (decorated) more frequently than you might think necessary, but in
those days they weren't. One room (at the Bay Horse) was papered once in about
fifteen years. Chimneys always smoked, and the smoking that went on – the ceilings
could set off a pale cream and finish mahogany brown – and eventually it was left
like that, that was part of the decor and showed the character of the place. At the
Bay Horse a lot of the lampshades were conical, white, like a Chinaman's hat –
there were some that had originally been shades for gas fittings. There were still the
original gas bracket arms, quite ornamental, but if you turned the gas on, it was still
there, you could have lit it.*

Noel Attree: *We had what we called the dram shop. And I remember going down
for some reason or other and thinking how cosy it was, big fire, and each side of
the fireplace there were those three sided – prisms do they call'em? Glass, there's
a name for 'em. And she had three or four altogether, they were hung up you see,
from a rod coming off the wall, about five or six inches. And the heat turned them
round, and you had all these colours: red, indigo, violet, yellow, orange, green,
blue going round, it was a lovely sight. My grandad died in April 1914, the floor
in the tap room, he laid that, and that floor is still there, one or two are cracked,,
but there's red and blue squares, if you look. It was always beautifully done, was
the singin' room – it was potted palms and some nice flowers. I never forget the
fireplace, it was a lovely marble with birds on – God knows what that would be
worth today, most magnificent looking thing. At the back of the singin' room was a
little door, it lead in to what was called the snug. Lovely canny litttle room was
that.*

Betty Harris: *The pub itself was austere (the Golden Lion, St. Sampsons Square,
in 1956). There was no luxury whatsover. The seats would be the type bolted to the
wall, they would be leatherette. The tables in the front bar would be wrought iron
ones. There was a snug, where you would see a chap with his lady, you know,
maybe somebody he shouldn't have been with. The door was always closed to the
snug. Upstairs there was a huge long room which they used to let out for
meetings, and there was a piano in it, and all sorts of bits and pieces. And the
room was drab, very drab. The life was drab then, there was no colour. People*

didn't wear light clothes, they didn't possess leisure clothes, it was drab, dark colours. I think they chose these dark colours because they were serviceable. You didn't get people going to the dry cleaners in those days, they didn't have washing machines.

Lily Grayson: *They had bells all round the pub* (the Phoenix), *on the wall behind the seats, what they could press, but nine times out of ten they just shouted. We allus waited on 'em, even in the bar. Nobody came up for their drinks.*

The 1960s saw a great change in the interiors of many public houses, many losing their character in the modernisation. Some landlords resisted the changes, some modified them to their own historical perspective, some welcomed them.

Sheila White: *The Jubilee had been modernised when we went in, and we didn't like it. It was*

42. The Phoenix, George Street. 1935.
(City of York Library)

when plastic first came in. They told us that before it had a beautiful counter, beautiful fixtures and fittings. It had a stone floor and they'd tiled it. And they'd done it up – and they did them wrong, didn't they? They got their homework wrong.

We got it all nicely smartened up (on moving to the Castle Howard Ox). *The only way I can describe the 'Ox' – it was like a little Victorian pub, and we had velvet seats and red carpets and decor done in a Victorian manner, because it was a coaching inn and should never, ever, have been modernised inside. They had a pot-bellied stove in the middle – well that did need taking out, you don't want those – but for other things, it should have been kept in keeping and made as it was. We had oil lamps put round the windows, and we had coach lamps put in the recesses, and we brought it back as far as we could to what it should have been. It was a quaint little place was the 'Ox'. It isn't now, 'cos they've pulled all the stables and the farrier's cottage down. And now it's like a modern pub, I'm told.*

John Greaves: *When they did alter it, they made a good alteration.* (Tetley's brewery at the Lion and Lamb). *It was good, we enjoyed it, it was sort of 'Olde Worlde'. Instead of having a bar and three or four rooms they opened it up and made a big lounge. And what was the top half of our cellar, an original cellar arch, like a vault, they incorporated that into the alterations, which I wanted them to do. They kept the old beams, the original beams. And they built a nice, big, stone fireplace in the front, with a dog grate, and I used to burn big logs, apple logs. It was really nice, and it attracted an awful lot of youngsters, it was the 'in' place if you know what I mean.*

Some changes were an 'alteration too far'.

John Greaves: *And after we left they altered it again. They altered its name, for some reason or other, to the 'Nickel and Dime'. The idea was to attract youngsters.* (The 'Nickel and Dime' was not a success and closed permanently within a short time of its renaming. After more than two hundred and fifty years of life as an inn and hotel, the teatowels went over the pumps forever.)

43. The Lion and Lamb, Blossom Street. 1980.   *(Hugh Murray)*

Some tenants worked hard, with few resources, to refurbish and bring new life into premises which had suffered from neglect.

Eve Briggs: *Solly Morris who used to have the White Swan* (in Piccadilly) *said, "Fancy buying a pig in a poke like that, you'll be in and out in six months"* (the Bay Horse in 1951). *I sez, "We'll see about that". We opened the smoke room – we'd no money, and I even cut up a black dress to make a pelmet – and me brother made a bar to go in it. We put coconut matting on the floor, we had little pineapple lamps on all the tables . . . and it got real popular, you know. We used to get all t'business people down there, Richardson the printer, Woodcock the baker and Dandy the baker. All good punters, you know, and touch wood, we never looked back.*

Although many public houses were, by today's standards, lacking decent standards of furnishing and amenities, they were still superior to what many customers had at home, and they did provide warmth, a modicum of comfort, and a break from the drudgery of everyday life.

Ron Powell: *Pubs often used to serve as the lounge of the house. People lived in two up and two down, big families, worked hard, came home, half a dozen kids, and the bloke was tired out. And you can take it he didn't have much money, but he'd go to the pub, spend thre'pence on a half of bitter, tuppence ha'penny on a pint of mild, sit there for an hour and a half and keep warm. It was peace he wanted, and the wife knew this. They* (pubs) *filled a social need in that respect.*

Fred Veitch: *You're talking of an era when there wouldn't be a lot of comfort. People didn't have three piece suites, they'd have wooden chairs in their houses, and I suppose the pub was a bit more of a better environment for 'em – they weren't using their own light and coal and that.*

4. A WOMAN'S PLACE?

Women have long been involved in the serving and brewing of beer. In medieval times the business of brewing was a process in which women were predominant, when they were known as 'ale wives'. When the ability to increase the shelf-life of beer became possible in the 16th century, and brewing became a business, rather than a cottage industry, ale wives disappeared from view. Until relatively recent times, employment opportunies for married women were very few indeed, but the running of licensed premises was one, with its natural combination of home and business, which they could undertake. In 1929 twenty seven women were licensees of the 159 fully licensed houses in the city, and ten were licensees of the twenty four beer houses, and although many of these were widows who continued with the licence on the death of their husbands, they very often ran the pub as efficiently as their now deceased spouses. Many of the pubs that had the husband's name above the door had so for convenience – it was easier for a man to obtain a licence. The husband would often carry out other employment whilst his wife ran the pub. Despite this, even fellow publicans were less than welcoming to the ladies in their

44. The elegantly dressed past presidents of the ladies' section of the L.V.A., gathered together at a function around 1970. Left to right: Mrs Powell, Stead, Fieldhouse, Furby, Fletcher, Holliday, Atha, and Flowers. *(Barbara Fletcher)*

midst, in the early part of this century. In November 1919, Mr. Edward Gretton's proposal at an L.V.A. meeting that, 'Ladies should be allowed to attend dinner', failed to get a seconder!

Noel Attree: *She went and took the 'Woolpack'* (the Woolpack hotel, Fawcett Street) *did me mother, but it was what was known as a 'drovers' pub' in those days, you know, lime washed ceiling's, flagged floors, wooden settles, and it was really . . . you couldn't believe it. I remember as a kiddie sitting on her knee, in the kitchen, having something to eat, and there were little mice flying about in the fireplace. You know it really was a shocker. But from what it was, she brought that pub up, from that, to one of the nicest, most well appointed pubs in York. She ran the pub on her own, actually. Me stepfather helped her out, but she was the guiding light of the pub, and good at it.*

Bob Barker: *I worked at Fulford Barracks, as a civil servant . . . wife ran it* (the Brown Cow) *during the day, I did it at night time and weekends.*

Joan Whitehead: *She was the manageress* (her mother at the Three Tuns) *and he* (her father) *used to come down on a night, if he wasn't working, and help her behind the bar.*

John Greaves: *She ran it on her own* (his mother at the Lion and Lamb during the First World War). *I suppose it was a hard job, you know. She had all these troops billeted on the premises, and in the house. The horses, the guns and God knows what else . . . the Flying Corps.*

Doreen Bolton: *He came home one night and I said, "Wally, I'm going to take a pub, I might as well be an ornament". And I went to my granny and said, "I want to take a pub, I'm not doing anything, I'm just like a carpet". And she took me down to Hunt's Brewery for an interview, and about a week later I got a letter saying would I go, and I got the 'Royal Oak'. Youngest landlady in Yorkshire I was. But Wally always kept his job on. He helped me every night like, but he always kept his job on.*

Of course, a husband and wife combination helped in providing a family atmosphere.

Ron Powell: *They worked in harness did landlords and their wives. Often the wife would be the more sympathetic person. If a man had lost his wife then the landlady said a few words, which happens today, in that sort of pub.*

John Greaves: *In those days people went into a pub and they stayed there, it was their home. The rents were quite reasonable in those days, before the breweries got too greedy, and they made a home of it. But now they're in and out, just sort of caretaking, you see.*

45. The Pack Horse Hotel, Micklegate. 1920s. *(Bill Stephenson)*

If a landlord or landlady died 'in harness' it was often a daughter who provided the strongest support in keeping the business going.

Doreen Greaves: *Once he died* (her father at the Pack Horse) *I said, "That's me finished, I'm not going to school anymore". It was after school leaving age, and I didn't. I don't know how my mother would have managed without us really.*

Mabel Wilson: *I was fourteen at Christmas and she died* (her mother) *a fortnight later. Yes, I took over the running of the house.*

Fred Veitch: *My eldest sister, Peg, she would be about fifteen or sixteen when we went to live there* (at the Five Lions) *and my Mother died very early on, and she took over the pub and was more or less the landlady.*

Pauline Worthy: *When my dad died I took over doing the banking, doing the books. I ran the pub with me mam.*

Women who ran pubs had to be strong and resourceful – combining this with an attractive personality did no harm!

Doreen Greaves: *We used to have to lift in crates of beer, pint cases of beer, and draymen had to wear rubber gloves to save their hands. And I remember lifting double pint cases of beer, wooden, two dozen bottles – the splinters you used to*

46. Kath Staines poses in a promotion for Moussec products in the York Arms, at the time she entered the 'Hostess with the Mostest' competition in 1956.

(Harry Atkin)

get in your hands! Lift 'em up, cart 'em in, and then they brought in plastic! I used to think, "Soft, these men".

Doreen Bolton: *She always got a licence did me granny, it was unusual for a lady to have a licence then* (in the 1910s). *She had two pubs at once did me granny: 'Barrack Tavern', where barracks is, and 'Ye Olde No. 5'. She was very, very strong.* (In 1911 Emma Gretton, Doreen's grandmother, held the Barrack Tavern in her husband's name, the Ye Olde No. 5 in her own).

Harry Atkins: *The Moussec traveller was visiting the York Arms and he was impressed by the manner in which my sister could deal with the clientele. And he suggested my sister go into a competition 'The hostest with the mostest' that was being held in London. And she came second, and this was reported in many of the newspapers of the time.* (There were 3,500 entrants to the competition, held in 1956).

Doreen Bolton: *I think me mam's pub was one of the most popular* (the King's Head in the 1920s), *she'd a lot of personality, had me mam.*

Eric Shaw: *Mrs. Bolton* (Doreen Bolton of the Royal Oak), *she loved to get dressed up. I remember her once coming in in a black dress. She looked quite stunning.*

Doreen Greaves: *Everybody called her 'Ma Brown'* (her mother at the Pack Horse), *everybody called her that. The blokes used to admire her intensely.*

Eve Briggs: *I was a mannequin for a while, and I used to give lectures on make-up and skin care. I met this woman off the stage, and she showed me how to put glitter on your eyes. I started doing that on Saturday night, you see. Every time I moved, people could see your eyes, and they used to be fascinated. I had people come from Hull one night. They said, "We've come all this way to see your eyes". I said, "I don't have it on on a Tuesday, wait a minute while I go and slap some on!"*

Although running a pub was a perfectly respectable occupation for a woman, being a female customer was a totally different matter. Some pubs would not allow unaccompanied women in at all, or restricted them to the passage, usually adjacent to the 'jug and bottle' serving hatch. Some would not allow them in the bar, and very rarely would a 'lady' enter the main room of a pub without a male escort. The licensees of sixteen public houses in the Fishergate area were allowed extension of hours on Cattle Market days, and they decided at a meeting at the Melbourne Hotel in March 1930 that, 'Licensees would refuse to serve local women during the hours of extension on market days'. Of course the term 'local women' may have been a euphemism for women of a certain profession, but certainly women in the period before the Second World War had to accept restrictions that would have proved unacceptable after its conclusion.

47. Eve Briggs behind the bar, at the Bay Horse, Marygate. c.1970.   *(Eve Briggs)*

From Miss Sturdy, an early contributor to the York Oral History Society archive, whose father was the tenant of the Victoria Hotel on Heslington Road before the First World War: *And I remember once, my dad came in and he said to my mother, "Did I see two women coming out of the front door? You know very well we don't serve women, we don't have women in pubs". And my mother said, "They've been to a funeral, they were wanting to recover, they were upset". And he said, "Well just remember, we don't have women in pubs".*

Sheila White: *I think years ago, I would say up to the war, I don't think many women went unaccompanied. They used to say that if a woman went into a pub on her own, she was going in to pick somebody up.*

Mabel Wilson: *Ladies didn't go in public houses on their own in the early days, they used to come in the passage for a drink to take out, and have one on their own. It was only to sit and talk when they were on their own, it was one way of putting the night in. They were never, never, allowed in the bar.*

Noel Attree: *Generally they were mature ladies with a family who'd call in, you know, the family up and away, grown, married. Maybe just called in to the 'bottle and jug' as it was called, to buy a jug of beer. They'd probably have half a beer as well. They'd bring a jug that maybe held three pints, and they used to ask for three pence of beer, a gill o'beer. "Give it a long pull, John, will yer", you know, so they* *got a bit more. They used to sit on a little settle there and have a drink, quietly. But you never saw a woman walk in* (the Red Lion) *on her own, not like you would today, oh no. And you never saw a woman in the tap room, never.*

Lela Norfolk: *We had a little snug, we called it the snug, and they'd* (women) *go in there* (at the Mount Hotel in the 1960s). *They're not seen in the passage, they'd just nip in. It was very quiet, so they weren't seen. 'Cos it was a bit of a disgrace like, in them days, for a woman to be in a pub without her husband. It was all right if she had her husband with her.*

Betty Harris: *A little area of the passage had blue seats,* (at the Golden Lion) *and there were always two or three little old ladies sitting there. They'd have been to the Home and Colonial, Lipton's, and all those other places, and they'd come in for their half of mild and loads of laughter.*

Lily Grayson: *The lads who worked in the cattle market went in the bar, and me dad, at first, wouldn't let women go in there. But then he realised that these women – who went potato pickin' – were more at ease in the bar, so he allowed them in. Most of the women were beer drinkers – they used to drink pints.*

Stan Leaf: *Mainly married couples . . . they used to come in with their wives* (at the Phoenix), *it was conducted on a proper footing. They soon found out they weren't allowed in, women* (alone).

There were however some women who would enter a pub or hotel without a male escort, usually females 'of a certain age', in groups, and often using the better class establishments, or coming out for special occasions. Surprisingly perhaps, even in Victorian times women would use public houses for meetings. In 1848 the 'Female Order of York Druidesses, White Rose of York Lodge' held their first tea party for sixty members and friends in the Leopard Inn, Coppergate.

48. Pauline Worthy (far right) enjoys a night out with other landlords daughters at an L.V.A. function in the 1950s. *(Pauline Worthy)*

John Greaves: *Going back a long way, when I was a kid, the little room, which was sort of classed as a private room, that's where the better class ladies used to go. I can picture quite a few now, the way they dressed, the more genteel ladies – the high frilled neck collars, the long black gown, always in black. They used to come in and have their little drops of port, and the odd sherry.*

Sheila White: *My Aunt Peggy used to put on those long, flowing voile dresses with scarves, and me mother used to get dressed up and they'd go to the Station Hotel. They'd have a coffee and chartreuse or a 'Green Goddess' in the resident's bar, because they were known, have one drink and come out.*

Doreen Bolton: *I used to have a lot of old dears on St. Patrick's Day, they used to put clean pinnies on. They'd start at the 'Oak', do Walmgate, and finish at the 'Oak'. They used to say, "We don't want any tuppence ha'penny today, Doreen, we want top shelf". 'Cos two and ha' pence was half a bitter you see. Top shelf, a drop of whisky, that used to be sevenpence.*

Some individual females did risk – or were beyond – the approbation of society, or used pubs for professional purposes. These were often the old, the non-conforming, or prostitutes.

Fred Veitch: *You very, very rarely saw a woman go in a pub on her own in those days* (the 1930s). *But there was one woman I can remember, a girl called Pat. I don't know how you would describe her nowadays, she was the type of woman that preferred men's company. She used to come in the bar and stand as one of the lads.*

Noel Attree: *I remember one dear old character, an Irish lady who used to come in – all they seemed to wear was a black apron and shawl – and she used to sit in the dram shop. And she'd buy a clay pipe, have half an ounce of thick twist, and her matches. And she'd sit there not speakin' to anybody, break this pipe stem in half, so it was a short stem, roll the 'bacca in her hands like a man, fill it and smoke it, and have a pint of beer.*

Pauline Worthy: *We had a prostitute who used to use our house* (the 'Talbot' around 1950.) *She was black haired, tightly taken back, parted in the middle, big, long, dangly earings. Very quiet, very clean, nice lady. Somebody would be drinkin' in the bar and nod across to her, and she'd nod back, and she'd put her's* (drink) *to one side, and they'd walk out. But it was all done very discreetly, everything was discreet.*

Doreen Bolton: *They used to have a right hectic Sunday dinnertime* (at the King's Head in the 1920s). *She used to get a lot of birds in, I would think that they were whores, on the quiet, I don't know. I used to call 'em all aunty. But they were all very nice.*

Vera Lyall: *You got a lot of these women came in* (prostitutes to the Lord Nelson in the late '50s). *There was one who was a regular customer. She once brought in a chap who had a pub, and she didn't half slate him. She got him to buy a bottle of gin and a bottle of something else and then she took him home and then when she came out at night she brought the stuff back and sold it. She was a really nice sort of person, very generous. If somebody had no money and she had, she'd give 'em half of it. There were loads in that area, in those days. They behaved themselves, you never got any trouble.*

Doug Dalton: *There was one lady who used to come in* (to the Greyhound Hotel in 1957). *She never picked any blokes up in front of us, but she'd follow one or two out, then she'd come back in again. I always remember, she used to have a cigarette in the corner of her mouth, and as soon as it went down there was one in the other side. She used to always have one of these big, white, frilly blouses on, she seemed to be falling out everywhere. Always plenty of make-up on, her hair dyed a horrible sort of auburny colour. She wasn't young, she was getting on a bit, she was a biggish woman. Never-the-less, one of the characters that went in the pub, you know.*

With the two World Wars came progressive social changes that were never fully reversed in peace time. Women were the main beneficiaries, their personal freedom increasing with each conflict.

Mabel Wilson: *Women started to come in more when the war was on* (into the Edward V11 during the First World War). *They used to have to stand in the passage. With it being war time the downstairs room was made into a ladies' room at night. It changed everything, it never reverted back. When I was at the theatre, ladies used to come in on their own and have a sherry at the bar. They would never have done that in days gone by.*

Sheila White: *I would say that up to the war* (the Second World War) *not many women went in unaccompanied, they'd maybe go in Saturday and Sunday with their husbands. But of course when the war came and the men went away, the women weren't going to sit at home, were they? They went out to work, so they wanted entertainment. They'd go to the dance and at the interval they used to wander into the pubs. The Albany dance hall, their dancers used to go into the White Swan, or the Half Moon. The De Grey Rooms, people out of there used to go to the little pubs – the Bootham Tavern, the White Horse and the Waggon and Horses.*

Pauline Worthy: *My grandfather would never have a woman in the public bar, you couldn't get over the threshold, but that changed as time went by.*

Eve Briggs: *I used to go in the Punch Bowl and the Starre* (during the Second World War) *when the blackouts were on, when I left work, in a group. I wouldn't*

49. The Waggon and Horses, Gillygate. 1930s.   *(City of York Library)*

go on my own even now. All the years I've been a publican, I wouldn't go in on my own.

During, and after, the Second World War, women were even starting to take part in pub games, and by the 1950s they had their own darts and domino competitions.

Barbara Fletcher: *Kath Coulson, Doris Stones and me started the darts off in York, for women, and it was the York Ladies Darts League, and it's been going thirty odd years. I used to go out on a bike, I used to go to all t'outlying villages and get a shilling from 'em – they used to pay a shilling a week for women's darts. It's fading badly now, 'cos ours is a double board, and they don't want a double board now, they want a treble board.*

Pauline Worthy: *I don't remember working girls coming in much, but the older generation did, the older ladies, to play dominoes. It was a social place for them* (the Talbot in the 1940s).

Gill Thompson: *We had a ladies' darts team, which was unusual for those days* (at the Edinboro Arms in the late 1950s, early 1960s). *There weren't many ladies' darts leagues.*

Sheila White: *They used to play fives and threes and dominoes, and darts* (at the Jubilee in the early 1960s). *We had a ladies 'A' and a 'B' team, and we used to go*

50. Mr. Richard Kincel, former landlord of the Brown Cow, Hope Street, presents the Kincel Cup to the winners, the ladies' darts team of the Bay Horse, Monkgate. 1958. *(David Atha)*

out to different places. We were in the country league, and we used to go out to them, we used to go in a bus.

But old habits die hard, and until very recently in traditional working class areas, men still resented women's presence and influence in pubs.

Lela Norfolk: *We had a corner where all the men collected* (at the Mount Hotel in the 1950s and 60s,) *where women didn't go in. They knew it was men only. You had to have a place like that. Some fellers wouldn't go drinkin' where women were about.*

Pauline Coldrick: *It wasn't 'til probably the late fifties that – maybe my mother – started saying, "They're* (women customers at the Frog Hall) *buying raffle tickets and should have something out of it". And so we used to run women's trips, and it was usually an evening out, when pub grub came in and country pubs were doing evening meals. And I think that there was quite a lot of resentment among certain of the older men. Again, it was that sort of area, a very chauvinistic attitude. And those things didn't die out in that area until very recently.*

51. A group of York landladies gathered on the steps of the Mansion House, York, with the Lord Mayor, Alderman William Horsman in 1940. The group contains many of the best known landladies of the day, including Mrs. Hardy, Powell, Fieldhouse, Waite, Melson, Goodhall, Gott, Furby, Fairburn, Boulton, Moore, Yorke, Shaw, Bush and Archer.

(Lily Grayson)

5. PUB CUSTOMERS

It's a truism that among every pub's customers there is a 'character', and often more than one. As the definition of such a person might be – 'outgoing, extrovert, eccentric', it is obvious why they should be drawn to frequent public houses. The public bar is a stage on which they can perform, with an audience ready to be entertained. In this chapter we hear of just a few of the men and women who brightened the lives of those around them.

Noel Attree: *We had one feller used to come, we called him 'Punch'. Do you remember Freddie Frinton, on the telly? How he used to have that cigarette? Well you would have thought that Freddie Frinton had've got his act from 'Punch', 'cos when he'd had two or three pints, that's just how he smoked a cigarette. He was always laughin' – but he had his threadbare cap and suit, you know, the old scarf, fastened under the braces. And he got this letter to go and see a solicitor, to hear something to his advantage. And they gave him £100 that was left* (in a will) *and they were paid in the old Bradbury notes,* (the nickname of pound notes of this period, the 1920s, named after the chief cashier of the Bank of England, whose signature appeared on the note). *And there was three of his pals went with him, and they called in the Garrick Head* (Petergate), *the Alexander* (Market Street), *and he bought half a dozen glasses from Woollen and Harwoods. And they got to Stubbs* (the ironmongers on Foss Bridge) *and they went in and bought a hip bath. So they walked in* (to the Red Lion) *with this bath, and he said to John* (John Davison), *"John, I want four pints of your best bitter, and four cigars for four hussars"* – I think they were in the Yorkshire Hussars in the First World War – *"And I want you to fill it* (the bath) *with beer, not up to t'top, leave it about six inches from t'top". And he did. And they took this up the back way, and a tram was comin', and they lowered t'bath right across the tramlines. And the tram feller stops you see, comes out – you should have heard the language! 'Punch' gave him a Woodbine and a pint: "Don't worry". 'Course the conductor comes along; "What's going on?" He has one. There's about half a dozen on, and they all sat having a drink and a puff. Can you imagine that happening today? Off they went, to t'top of 'Clock'* (the Clock public house) *yard, put it down at t'top, had a chair round and their Woodbines, 'Sporting Pink', and Matty Myers the bookmaker not far away. Spent all afternoon having a drink, having a bet. Thought it was heaven!*

Harry Atkin: *One dear lady, I always used to treat her with respect, and called her Mrs. R. She was a widow, and her favourite tipple was several bottles of Guinness. I well recall one visit, when she was partaking of the Guinness, when I was looking after the pub because my brother-in-law, Sid, and my sister, were having a night out. Several of Sid's ex-police colleagues had come over to see him*

52. The Garrick's Head, Petergate, in the early part of this century. *(John Terry)*

53. The Clock Inn, Walmgate. 1935. *(City of York Library)*

and I explained the situation to them. One chap who was with them was particularly short in stature, and Mrs. R. was obviously intrigued, and she made the remark that he wouldn't be in the police force because of his lack of stature, and he agreed, so the lady looked up at him and said, "I didn't think you'd be a policeman, because looking at you, you'd have to stand on a hankie to look up a duck's arse".

Pauline Coldrick: *Jockey Giles, who you've heard about, he was a coal merchant, a bookie, a bit of this, a bit of that, wheeling and dealing. He was a real Del Boy. He must have been the biggest character in York, Jockey. Leading light in all the pub social activities – I'm talking about in the early days, 1949/50 – and he organised what he called the shaving club. The men used to come in on a Sunday morning in false beards, some didn't have beards and would have had a shave. They were fined according to . . . they were fined anyway, either they'd had too close a shave or they hadn't had a shave. He organised silly walking matches where they all got dressed up or pushed prams and this sort of thing. He'd see how far he could go, always a joke, dry humour. Then there was a woman (customer at the Frog Hall.) She was known as Annie Cox, a little old lady who looked like Old Mother Riley. And she had the most raucous laugh, and she would*

54. Annie Cox entertains at the Frog Hall, Layerthorpe. c.1970.   *(Pauline Coldrick)*

entertain everybody in the passage. For half a pint of beer you could have your evening's entertainment. And she always had a clean pinafore on over her dress, or whatever. And she'd dance and throw her skirt up, and show her bloomers and all this, and sing. A real character was Annie.

Mabel Wilson: *It was a thing on at the 'Empire', like a talent contest, and we pulled Jimmy Iveson's leg, and we all went to have a laugh, and he went as a female. They called him 'Snuffy' Iveson, because he was always taking snuff, and he took this snuff out because he forgot where he was. They brought the police, 'cos they thought he was trying to be a woman. Now it's legal, but not in those days* (around 1920). *The police didn't say anything, so he was all right. They used to have things like that. One Sunday night they got Jimmy Sanderson to go as the Lord Mayor of York in an open carriage, with this chain – there wasn't the games there are now, you see.*

Lily Grayson: *The only woman who would come in on her own* (to the Phoenix) *was Jeff Quigley's mother, Mary Ann. She used to come dashin' into the pub and say to me dad, "Give us a whisky Brad, I don't think I'll last much longer" – a few drinks later she was dancin' on the table tops! She lived for years after that. She was a real character; so was Geoff, he used to dance on the tables, do the Horn-pipe – he was very good. We had some good nights you know.*

The city's pubs also attracted the actors and entertainers who were appearing at local venues.

Harry Atkin: *I was very friendly with Jimmy Beck (*the actor who played the 'spiv', Walker, in the T.V. series 'Dad's Army'). *We had this standing joke between us; we were supposed to go swimming every morning in the River Ouse at quarter to seven. We always used to come up with something fresh about this early morning swim: "By, as I dived in, the ice just scraped my chest!" Other people who come to mind are Fred Trueman, and he was very friendly with John Gregson. Sir John Barbirolli, he used to pop in from time to time. I do recall John Leyton (*an actor and pop singer famous in the 1960s) *coming in and we were swamped with young girls, after his autograph. From the acting fraternity, Jean Alexander comes to mind – Hilda Ogden in 'Coronation Street' – and Judi Dench was a regular.*

Pauline Worthy: *Gracie Fields stayed there when she was young* (at the Talbot). *And me mother remembers Gracie Fields in tears, telling me grandmother she'd broken this bowl that was in the bedroom. I remember as a kiddie that anybody who came to the Empire theatre would come along to the Talbot. Albert Modley used to come, and he'd stand in our bar, and he used to give a turn.*

Gill Thompson: *With being so close* (to the Rialto cinema, which was famous for its Sunday night pop concerts) *the ones at the bottom of the bill would always come and stay with us: Cliff Richard, Mick Jagger, Gary Glitter, Shane Fenton, Engelbert Humperdinck when he was Gerry Dorsey, Roy Orbison, the Shadows.*

55. Jessie and Harry Ashton Campbell, son Frank and cousin Ruth Inglis gather together with customers at the York Arms. 1930s. *(Barry Grayson)*

56. Same pub, different era. Less restrained customers having a good time at the York Arms.
1960s. *(Harry Atkin)*

The only person that stayed with us when they got near the top was Roy Orbison.
None of them were temperamental, they were all really lovely. The only thing we
did find strange was that Brian Jones slept with his hat on, we thought that very
strange.

Doreen Bolton: *Michael Rennie, Helen Christie, Raymond Francis, John Gabriel,*
they all used to come in to t'Oak. I used to go in t'Museum Gardens on an
afternoon, and they used to learn their parts and say 'em to me, did repertory
company.

But even the famous had to obey the rules:

Doreen Greaves: *We didn't allow singing,* (in the Lion and Lamb) *and I was*
getting ready, and I thought, "I can hear singing". And I rushed into the bar, and
I could hear 'twangle, twangle, twangle', you know, and the place was as quiet as
a mouse. And I rushed round, and I said to this lad, "You can put that away, we
don't let anybody twangle a banjo in here". And there was a ghastly hush, and me
son, who was behind the bar said, "Oh mother!" I said, "Don't you mother me,
that's the rules". He said, "Mother, that's Lindisfarne". And I'd chucked 'em out!

The public house was always a place for meetings – trade union, masonic, sporting
club, all were welcome. The English publican has a long tradition of tolerance to his

57. Sometimes pubs could get more customers than they bargained for! Troops billeted at the Lion and Lamb in 1916. *(John Greaves)*

customers. As the name implies, licensed premises were there for the public to use. If they were reasonably sober, kept their own counsel and were able to pay their way, very few were turned away. Customers included the sad, the tired, the old, the lonely, the odd, the eccentric, the criminal, the observer, the outsider, as well as the gregarious, and the fashionable.

Ron Powell: *Upstairs, on the first floor of the house, was the club room. Meeting there* (the Bay Horse, Blossom Street) *was the 'Royal Antideluvian Order of Buffaloes'. They were very secretive, a bit like the masons, they used to wear regalia similar to the masons. They had various officers, and the door to the club room had a little trap, a little door, about six inches square. And the official in charge of that, anybody who knocked at the door, he looked through, and if he recognised a brother, he was admitted. Also meeting in the club room was the Scarcroft Bowling Club, although ultimately they got their own pavilion. The Scarcroft Flying Club, they were a society that ran racing pigeons, the Bishopthorpe Road Angler's Club, and the Amalgamated Association of Joiners and Woodworkers, they met once a fortnight. They used to get charged five shillings for the use of the room and a fire in winter.*

Doreen Bolton: *There'd be nobody in at half past five, I was upstairs talking to Wal' while he was having his tea, and I heard t'door go. I came downstairs, there* *was a feller fryin' kippers on a shovel, on t'fire. He was! You have some funny experiences in pubs.*

Doug Dalton: *We used to have one man come in, used to dress like a woman, and always sit at the bar heavily made up. Harmless, sat in a corner, just drinkin'. That was his way of life, he just used to sit there, drink his beer. Pint after pint after pint.*

Noel Attree: *There was quite a number* (of customers) *who stuck to one pub. They'd come in and have a pint, and they'd have their pipe or Woodbines. And they'd be sat in a corner, and they'd maybe not utter one word. They'd maybe get through five or six pints of beer, just nice and steady ploddin', and then go. They wasn't in the company, never heard 'em speak. What enjoyment they got out of the beer I don't know.*

Eric Shaw: *There was an old feller used to come in, me dad called him Russ. He'd nowhere to go. I remember he used to be first in at half past five, and there's many a time I've seen him come in absolutely drenched from t'pouring rain. And he'd maybe be the only one in 'til seven o'clock and he'd sit as close as he could to that fire, trying to dry out, maybe half a pint with him, that's all.*

Fred Veitch: *We used to do bed and beakfast, and there was one guy, he had a regimental tie, and could have been an ex-army officer. He came and stayed two or three nights, and each night he used to leave his shoes outside the bedroom door. Well me dad cleaned 'em, and he buggered off without paying. I remember me mam and dad telling that tale time and time again, "It was bad enough him leaving without paying, but I cleaned his bloody shoes!"*

There used to be a French onion man came over every year, lived in one of the garages at the bottom of the Five Lions yard. He had a camp bed with a primus stove, and a bike with a pole with his onions on. Must have used the pub toilets I suppose, where he washed and that. Couldn't speak very good English, but he got by all right.

Noel Attree: *Tom Bell came in this particular night, and he put his Woodbine in – maybe have two or three drags on his Woodbine and put it out, they used to make it last then, that was when Woodbines were five for tuppence, ten for fourpence – and he was going to get a light from the fire, and it wasn't there you see. So my Uncle John gave him a light, and he says, "You've got no fire tonight then?" Anyway he went missing, and we wondered where he'd gone, and he came back, did Tom, with paper, sticks and a bucket of coal, and he made his own fire.*

Of course the backbone of every pub is its 'regular', some who became almost part of the family. The pub was also a place where, on a lunchtime, tradesmen and business men met to relax, or talk 'shop', and where, maybe, deals could be struck. Pubs were also places where like-minded people would come together.

Pauline Worthy: *The people who came were like my family. They didn't come in the pub one night and then go somewhere else. They came to the Talbot. That was their place, yes. Workmen from the Gas Company used to come in. Myer's and Burnell's had a garage at the bottom of Swinegate, they used to come in. Bellamy's, painters and decorators, they were in Swinegate. Next door to us was the fruiterers, Hetherington's. Dodsworth's painters, they were in St. Sampson's Square, they used to come in. People from around – Bill Hesp, Dick Joy, they were businessmen, they came in. Stood in a certain place, had a certain drink, doffed their hats, and they went.*

Barry Grayson: *We knew about the gays, and I never, ever, discouraged it. I say that because they became the people I meet now as personal friends. They were nice people. What I liked about the pub was the intelligent repartee we had. I don't mind talking about football, or golf, but we used to talk about theology . . . anything. And we had this most marvellous little book rank, which had got built up over the years, which covered the whole bar. If anybody asked a question, we could probably find it amongst this pile of books. It was marvellous, it was a different pub. We were the first people to have punk rockers in, my son was a drummer, and the people he knew started to drift in. And I started looking round, and there were coxcombs, and pink hair and green hair. Then there were ten, then there were twenty, they were in every night. And I was saying to myself, "I'm too old for this". They were another group that was maligned because of their funny hairdos. I've seen 'em with coxcombs a foot high, going right the way back, and one bloke had to duck coming through the door. And they were spiky, like unicorns, and all the leather. I just used to go home and have a laugh. But we never had any trouble. I used to say, "I know that you're all smoking pot, or doing something or other, but don't do it in here. This is your pub, as well as mine, it's one place you can come where you don't get harassed. So look after the place, because if you get done, I get done. That way you are goin' to go". And I must admit there were only three occasions that I can actually say . . . I found someone smoking pot one night, and I took him by the neck and hurled him through the door.*

Fred Veitch: Now old Mr. Ellerker (Ellerker's rope and harness shop was nearly opposite the Five Lions), *I can remember him. He had his own chair in the smoke room, did Mr. Ellerker. In those days people had their own pubs. In the late '30s, when they started doing away with the old terraces in Walmgate, you know, moving 'em out, the men still came back to their own haunts. It would die out eventually. Sunday lunch time me dad always shut the pub at two o'clock. And usually there would be a couple of customers who lived on their own, having their dinner with us upstairs.*

Doug Dalton: *One old chap, he'd been coming in for more years than I care to remember. He was the editor, or a sub editor, at the Yorkshire Evening Press. He*

58. A bowler hatted Mr. Ellerker is one of the customers about to set out on a Five Lions trip in 1937. Landlord Peter Veitch is third from the right on the front row, with son Fred beside him. *(Fred Veitch)*

was a hell of a size, he must have weighed eighteen stones. He always used to eat three pork pies and have two pints of beer, every lunch time. And he used to come in on his way home and have the same. You could always tell what he had eaten by what was on the front of his shirt, tie, and jacket.

Eric Shaw: *They were nearly all regulars* (in the Angler's Arms in the 1930s). *We saw 'em every day of the week. Some of the old men, they'd be there on a dinnertime, you know. There was one feller who used to come in, he was black bright; he was a chimney sweep. It didn't matter how many baths he had, he was ingrained with soot, he was just black. And he'd come in, he'd chew this real black tobacco. It was wrapped up in like a string, and he'd sit chewin' this – that's when the spittoons came in that I was telling you about – and he'd sit there all day.*

Gill Thompson: *'Uncle Tommy', we used to call him. He was a farmer, he actually came to eat with us, became one of the family, and had his tea with us on Monday, Wednesday and Saturday.*

Doreen Bolton: *There was one room* (at the Royal Oak) *you could have got four double beds in, I used to call it t'drunks room. I used to put drunks in it, if they got too much, if they'd had too much to drink and they were ridin' a bike. I didn't let them go home on the bike, I used to put them to bed.*

59. The Edinboro Arms, before it became the Edinburgh Arms. 1960s.   *(Gill Thompson)*

Not all customers were regulars of course, some were visitors to the City. During race meetings public houses on the route to the Knavesmire from the railway station were particularly busy. Race crowds were always colourful and included beggars, ruffians, rogues, tipsters, and entertainers, as well as those just intent on having a good day out.

John Greaves: *The races? It was just like something out of a Hogarth painting. I couldn't stand it nowadays. They used to use the yard as a park, and they used to come staggering back from the races full of booze. There was no transport much in those days, and they used to come to a meeting and stay three days. They used to come in drinking, but as fast as you got rid of some, some more used to come in. People would do anything for money in them days. There was one chappie had white, curly, hair and he could clench his fist and put his whole fist in his mouth. I've seen a chap with no arms or legs come in on a skateboard, people pushing him around, begging.*

Ron Powell: *Spittoons eventually went out of fashion, with the exception of race days, the May and August days of the races, they were brought out then. In those days the race 'hangers on' were a pretty scruffy lot, but their money went in the till just like everybody else's. On race days it was absolute murder! Everybody came by train in those days* (the 1930s). *Trains used to arrive at York Station at ten minute intervals, from about half past ten onwards. The kitchen had a big wide* *window which used to slide up, with the kitchen table in front and two massive enamel jugs, one fillled with bitter, and one with mild and it was poured out of the jug. They used to sit on upturned beer boxes, or stand, and that was the backyard business. They always had a nine gallon firkin set on one side, and that came straight from the wood, but that only happened on race days. They used to have a board outside which said, 'Last pub to the course'. And a hundred yards further up on the other side of the road the Mount Hotel had a board saying, 'Last house to the course!' One thing I remember about the races: there used to be lots and lots of musicians come – some were pretty good players. One man used to wear a sailor's hat, white with gold braid round it, he used to play the banjo, he was very good. There was a man, he was an albino, he used to come round. His features were negroid, his hair was white and his complexion was very pale pink. He had a walking stick with a knob on the end, and he used to whistle. His gimmick used to be that he used to hit his head on the side of his stick, and according to where it hit his skull it produced a different note. He made a fearful noise, it must have been a hard way to make a living! There was always blind men, always with their dogs, they couldn't sing, but they were there for the coppers. They all used to*

60. The Bay Horse, Blossom Street. *(City of York Library)*

come in the pub, and they used to want to play in the pub, but we used to say, "We haven't got a music license, it's against the law", which it was.

Harry Atkin: *I well remember on race days* (in the 1930s) *people came by train. And there were so many special trains that even York Station couldn't cope – they had an excursion station close to Holgate Bridge. When the passengers were off-loaded most of them would walk down Holgate Road in droves, literally in hundreds. And to cope with the extra clientele the proprietor of the Crystal Palace used to put trestle tables and forms outside, for the extra clientele to partake of the beverages.*

Betty Harris: *Another huge thing about the the Woodman pub was the race days, that was folklore in Bishopthorpe, because on Ebor day we would have as many as twelve coaches for that little pub. We took some money on those days, and believe me, we needed it. We had our stall set out, it was a big deal; it was cups of tea and sandwiches at the back door and, of course, drinks at the front. I can still remember Kevin* (her son) *coming home from school and having to pitch in. We worked our socks off on race days.*

Mabel Wilson: *They weren't supposed to* (bet in the Edward V11 in the 1910s/1920s) *but of course they did. I was the bookie's runner, because they could trust me. We were the last pub to the racecourse – they made the Knavesmire* (hotel) *and the Winning Post* (public house) *later on – so you can imagine what we were like, it was a nightmare. We had maybe six or seven serving. They'd be drinking next to the urinal, anywhere. All down the streets off Nunnery Lane they used to take in bookies, because in those days bookies didn't go away, they stayed for three days. Nunnery Lane was chock-a-block with them. 'Prince Monolulu'* (a famous racing tipster) *he used to come in, "I've got a horse"* (a well known phrase shouted by the 'Prince').

Noel Attree remembers 'Prince Monolulu,' who dressed as an African prince: "*I went in* (the newsagents in Nessgate) *and little Harry was behind the counter, and I saw him looking over me shoulder, and I said, "What's up Harry?" He sez, "There's that feller over there, Noel, Prince Monolulu. He frightens me to death". "Why?" " Well you know, he's big, and he's black . . . " In those days there was no fly sprays, there was the old flypaper, and it was covered in sticky stuff each side, and you hung them up. And there were about three or four of these hung up in the shop, you see. Well sure enough Prince Monolulu come in, and what happens? He got his feathers stuck on the flypapers, didn't he? And you've never heard such language in all your life! Poor little Harry was under the counter. Oh! he was carrying on. Whether he bought owt or not I don't know, but it was a bit of excitement for a few seconds.*

61. Eve Briggs is one of the engrossed racegoers at the August meeting of York Races. 1947.

(*Eve Briggs*)

6. THE GAMES PEOPLE PLAYED

Games have long been a feature of pub life. In York, in this century, darts and dominoes have been predominant. These games were generally tolerated by the authorities as they were considered social, rather than gambling, activities, but even the playing of dominoes could, at times, be stopped by the police. In January 1928 at a Licensed Victuallers meeting Mr. Edgar complained, "that the police had stopped the playing of dominoes at the Burn's Hotel, " and asked, "Was this an action the police could enforce?" And in the 1920s the playing of games on licensed premises on a Sunday was not allowed, and a warning to that effect was sent to all L.V.A. members. By the 1920s, domino and dart matches were becoming a regular feature of pub life, and games leagues were formed by all the major breweries. Card games, with the exception of cribbage, were not allowed.

Attempts to introduce other games usually failed, the heavy hand of the law stifling any activity that might involve gambling. A Licensed Victualler's Committee meeting held at the Old Grey Mare in November 1933 recorded, 'Mr Backhouse made a statement as to the installation of pin bagatelle tables in three premises, and that the Chief Constable had stated that the licensees were saddled with the responsibility of preventing gambling. The brewers therefore decided that the tables should be removed'. There were other games that were popular with York's drinking fraternity, but which gradually fell out of favour and were little played after the Second World War. These included 'tippet', a simple game of bluff played between two three-man teams, and 'brasses' a game very similar to quoits. Brasses was a very popular game, and there was a flourishing brasses league, with matches played between competing working men's clubs, as well as amongst the customers in the city's pubs. In 1909 there were six teams competing in the York and District Licence Holders Brasses League, and in 1924 there were eight teams in the York Clubs and Institute Brasses League.

Ron Powell: *In the Bay Horse there was dominoes but nothing else. They could play cribbage, apparently in pubs. There used to be, sometimes, 'fives and threes', but mostly single line dominoes. They were expert, and knew what had gone, and what hadn't gone. It's a game of chance, and a novice can beat an expert, but over the night the expert won the money. They were only playing penny a corner, something like that.*

Don Nixon: *A lot of pubs had skittles, but it was just table top skittles, the one with the swinging ball. The Marcia at Bishopthorpe, they were brilliant at it in there* (in the 1960s). *Bar billiards went down very well, the one with the cones. The pub I remember a lot of us young ones used to play bar billiards in, was the Starre in Stonegate* (in the 1950s).

62. Even the great and the good can enjoy a game of darts! The Sheriff of York, Keith Wood, throws, whilst Lord Mayor Philip Booth looks on, at the Londesbro Hotel. 1982.

(Barbara Fletcher)

Eric Shaw: *They never played cards* (in the Angler's Arms), *all they did was darts and dominoes and fives and threes on t'domino board. There was never any gambling going on. He used to have proper wooden dart boards. We had two on the go, one was in soak – they had to be soaked to keep 'em soft – the other one, the men would be playing on. We never had trebles, me dad always told me that trebles was a southern game. It was just doubles and one hole for the bull, there wasn't a twenty five.*

Vera Lyall: *Twice a week we had darts on* (at the Three Cranes) *and you had to put a spread on each time. Used to be quite a do at one time, when they came from any of the villages. If they were playing in one of those leagues, they used to bring a bus load.*

Bob Barker: *We played darts, we had a ladies team and a men's. The ladies team won every trophy there was. All the Romanies played for 'em, and my God they can play darts, they're good. They won the singles, pairs, the championship, the fours. I was sick of cleaning t'cups on t'shelf! And they could hold their beer as*

63. Landlady Mrs.Pam Barker (far right) at the Brown Cow with the ladies' darts team. 1969.

(Bob Barker)

well. The more they drank, the better they played darts! And one used to say, "If you beat me, I'll put a curse on you!" And they used to fall for it you know – she was only joking! They were a lovely crowd. My wife used to go out with them, I used to go with the lads.

Arthur Briggs: *I had bar billiards in there* (the Bay Horse, Marygate) *but I had it taken out. We had it near the dart board, I wanted to join the darts league, so I got rid of t'bar billiards table.*

Doreen Greaves: *Shove ha'penny?* He had a big piece of slate, (her father at the Pack Horse in the 1930s) *and he had it made into this board. It was a brilliant game was that. There was a long board with lines across, you pushed the ha'penny with the palm of your hand. You shoved it up the board and wherever it landed in certain bands, you got points.*

Noel Attree: *I liked the old Red Lion, it was a grand pub. In the tap room you could play dominoes, you could play darts. You couldn't play on Sunday, and they were never allowed cards, but you could play 'tippit'. You used to have a little* button about the size of an old fashioned sixpence, you could buy these. I think they were made by somebody who probably worked at the railway, I think they were made in metal and had 'tippet' printed on. What you did, you got three men on one side, and three on the other, of the oblong, old fashioned, table, and the one in the middle used to 'work the button', as they called it. He'd tap the button in the middle of the table, and you'd go underneath the table (with your hands) and he'd move the button about and drop it into somebody's hand – or maybe he'd keep it himself. Then all of a sudden he'd 'up', and you'd clench your fists and you'd put them on the table. And whoever's turn it was (on the team opposite) had to find the button. And what they used to do was point, and say, 'Button', and they had a peg board, and if it wasn't there, you'd put that down . . . you used to play up to the end, whoever got to the end, then there were three pints of beer.

And on a Sunday afternoon you could play 'brasses'. By the back door at the Red Lion you could see a square piece of concrete, what would it be . . . two by two? (two x two feet). It was a clay pit and in the centre there was a metal rod, with a sort of 'staple' on the top. And your brasses were – imagine a tea cake cut in half – and they were made of metal. And you used to throw these, to knock this staple off this iron (metal rod). And they used to mark up (the scores) on the blackboard outside. That was played for beer as well.

Ron Powell: *There was an outhouse* (at the Bay Horse, Blossom Street) *called the brass room. Before I was born, or just after, they did used to play brasses in there. It's similar to quoits; they had cast iron discs, which were concave and reasonably heavy, and clay pits which were kept watered, and they put a marker in. And you had to hurl these* (discs) *as you would a discus from one end of the room to the other, and the nearest to the pin, or if you hit the pin, that was it. And back in about 1950 there was an old chap on television, Fyfe Robertson, and he'd heard of it. And they had this other bloke and my father on, and they had a demonstration throw on television to show people what it was like.*

7. ENTERTAINMENTS AND DIVERSIONS

Until recent times entertainment on licensed premises was generally basic, the piano being the major source of musical entertainment. Pubs were places to drink in, and except for games, landlords generally didn't see it as their remit to supply any other need. Authority saw the provision of entertainment as a possible source of public disorder, and many national and local laws were introduced to keep this possibility to a minimum. Licenses were required when music was a 'systematic entertainment' (casual music was not objected to, and was legal) and in 1924 a report in the Yorkshire Gazette stated that: 'Licensees in the City are loyally abiding by the recent magistrates' decision that women pianists must not play in the houses'. And at an L.V.A. committe meeting held at the Beeswing Hotel in March 1935, the secretary read a letter from Mr. Pickard of the Ouse Bridge Inn complaining that, 'the police had warned him against using a gramophone on the premises'. A further restriction on the granting of a music licence was the size of the room in which the entertainment was to take place. It had to be a minimum of five hundred square feet, and ten feet high. The 'Performing Right Act' even made the playing of the wireless in public rooms illegal, without the payment of an ever increasing annual fee.

It's fair to say that the authorities were determined that the 'wild' pre First World War days, when riotous behaviour was common on licensed premises, would not return, and laid a restrictive hand on any entertainment that they considered might encourage improper behaviour. In 1935 York was the only place in Yorkshire where no female artistes were allowed to perform on licensed premises. This meant that York pubs were generally places where the entertainment was simple, homespun, and unsophisticated, and the atmosphere – with some notable exceptions! – was comparatively restrained and the customers generally well behaved. However, with the coming of a second World War and its aftermath, the pendulum swung again.

Eric Shaw: *When husbands wanted to join their wives* (in the Angler's Arms in the 1930s), *they'd go into t'back room where t'piano was, under the staircase, and they'd start and have a sing song. It was never licensed for music but they always had a piano. Whoever could play t'piano played it, and that was it. Mrs. Woodcock, she was a bit of a singer, she could hit the high notes, and somebody would get on the piano and she'd get crackin'. They had some good nights in there. There was another old feller used to come in, he used to play the banjo and sing all t'old wartime songs, you know. If a soldier or Air Force man came in and he could play the piano, well it was open to anybody to have a go. One or two people who were on at t'Empire used to come in. One bloke brought a piano accordion in – not heavy going.*

Doreen Bolton: *Will Douglass at the Alexander, that's where Boots chemist is now, he used to have entertainment, piano and drums. I used to have a pianist, but*

64. Dot and Charlie Greaves, mother and father of John, at The Lion and Lamb. 1960s.

(John Greaves)

going back before my time (as landlady at the Royal Oak from 1938), *I can only remember the Alexander – not like it is now, with all that bloody noise!*

John Greaves: *We had a piano, my mother played* (at the Lion and Lamb). *She didn't play a lot from music, but she really was a good pianist. She played practically until she was eighty. The customers used to come in and they all used to sit together and sing songs, and one would get up and do a bit. But you know, there was no television in those days, and the customers in the public bar made their own enjoyment. They did all kinds of things to amuse themselves, and that was their night out. Then of course the Performing Rights came into being, I think it was two pounds a year. You couldn't even listen to your own radio behind the counter if the public could hear it, you had to pay Performing Rights for that.*

Sheila White: *At the 'Vic' on Cemetery Road* (the Victoria Hotel in the 1940s) *there were two sisters, Gladys and Myra Partridge. They had beautiful voices, they used to entertain all night, singing all the songs that were popular, and everybody joined in. It was a singsong on a Friday and Saturday night. So the karaoke is only the modern way of doing the entertainment that was in pubs.*

94

Of course things were always that bit livelier in Walmgate before the Second World War!

Fred Veitch: *You've got to remember that pubs in those days* (pre Second World War) *were the centre of entertainment. I can remember acrobats coming in and doing their turns, handstands and cartwheels and all that. You always had accordions and banjoes in the Five Lions, oh yes, and every night. Nearly all the pubs of any size would have a pianist, and you would pay the pianist, but these accordions, ukeleles, violins, just went round with a hat. I can remember me dad buyin' a radiogram before the war, and you had eight records that used to drop down, and I used to have to put the records on.*

Lily Grayson: *There used to be a man called Joe Carter, he used to come in with one of those penny whistles, and he always sat with his knees right up to t'fire – the' was open fires, you know. And some lads that sang there had beautiful voices, these Irish lads, they used to sing on their own. We had some real good sing-songs, you know. It allus ended up dancin' – singin' Nellie Dean as they were goin' home! It used to wake us up when we were small, but when we got grown up and moved away I found it difficult to sleep because it was so quiet.*

Noel Attree: *My grandma* (at the Red Lion post World War One) *used to advertise for a lady pianist in the 'Stage', when it was just after pantomime, their quiet time. She got her own room, free board and lodging, and a wage on top, so she did all right, until the summertime came. You never saw 'em in the summer, that was the . . . what was called the pierrot show, or any entertainment at the seaside. She played most nights, until, if you wanted a singing licence you had to be of a certain cubic capacity, and all that sort of thing. Whether that finished it or not I don't know. People came from all around, you know, Saturdays, Sundays, to the singin' room, it was always full. Have a natter, listen to a bit of nice music and somebody singin', it was very nice.*

Often the landlord or landlady themselves provided the entertainment.

Ron Powell: *My grandfather* (at the Bay Horse) *was always one for a gamble. One of his favourite gambles, he'd race a man over 50 yards, but he wanted a yard start. And these young blokes would take him on, but my grandfather was bigger than me, and he used to choose the Press Office passage, Commonhall Lane. And of course me grandfather had a yard start, and nobody could get past him!*

Sheila White: *Bill Fairless, a landlord before us at the 'Ox', weighed 25 stones, and he had the biggest waistcoat in York, and he had pockets in it. And he used to put the glasses in his waistcoat pockets and walk round with them, just for fun. There was big Billy Bridges, we used to call him boy, he was a captain at sea. He*

95

65. The Old Malt Shovel pub in Walmgate in the 1940s, when the area was in decline.

was at the 'Clock', next to Marks and Spencers. He used to stand on the step with his captain's hat on and salute people as they went by. Then there was Doris Stones, she used to have the Waggon and Horses, and she used to have the most fantastic hats, like the ones you see at Ladies Day at Ascot. And she used to serve behind the bar with them on. Her hair was platinum blond, with a bun at the back. She could keep you alive, she had a real patter about her. She didn't care what she said, or who she said it to, but everybody loved her.

Don Nixon: *I was born in the Groves, and I was three years old, and there was a little corner shop, almost opposite the Castle Howard Ox, and I went down for some sweets,*

66. Don Nixon was landlord of the Castle Howard Ox in the 1980s. Here he is pictured in the pub doorway, on the right, in 1985, when his 'five and threes' domino team were winners of a national competition, winning £2,000. Team captain Malcolm Hick is seen holding the dominoes. *(Don Nixon)*

and I came running home and said, 'I've just seen a giant'. And there's a chap called Bill Fairless, he was the licensee, and he stood in the doorway, and there was no way to get past him. He was the biggest man I've seen in my life. He used to be able to put six pint glasses in his waistcoat pocket. They called it Bill Fairless's pub.

Doreen Bolton: *I used to love to go to see my Uncle Eddie* (Edward Gretton). *He had the Grapes at the top of King Street. He was a ventriloquist, and he could do it right good.*

Eve Briggs: *I used to sing, I used to play the accordion. They used to say,"Come on Eve, give us a song". I used to have background music, I used to mimic people.* And if mine host host didn't provide the entertainment there were other members of the household who might . . .

Edith Keech: *I bought Ena* (Ena Davison, who took over the tenancy of the Minster Inn on her mother's death in 1944) *a parrot, which was kept behind the bar. It would call out, "Time gentlemen please" and when you put your coat on, "Cheerio".* (Charlie the parrot is still alive and well).

On one occasion the entertainment provided was unexpected!

Van Wilson: *Doris Stones was quite a character. At one time she was the landlady of the White Horse in Bootham, and my mum helped her out in the bar there for a bit, and there's a famous incident when my mum was working there: My mum was in the bar – this was in the morning before they opened – and this rep came and wanted to see Doris, and my mother said, "O.K, I'll just shout her, she won't be long, she's in the bath". So she shouted up, and Doris came down into the bar – knowing he was there – completely naked, and just walked in, not fazed at all: "Yes, can I help you?" He was so taken aback! My mum was quite used to this behaviour, or unsurprised by it should I say. Doris was quite a curvaceous woman, so this guy nearly passed out! And that was the sort of person she was, she just didn't bother about what other people thought. She was very popular.*

As ever, wartime – and its aftermath – brought social changes. Post war full employment meant that the working man had money to spend, many more women were going out to work, and both sexes wanted more from life than their parents had. This was reflected in the entertainment provided on licensed premises, which became wide-ranging and professional, and with advances in technology, more sophisticated. However, the acceptance of television, for example, initially varied from pub to pub.

Pauline Worthy: *If there was boxing on the radio* (at the Talbot in the late 1940s) *– Bruce Woodcock perhaps – they would all go upstairs and listen on the landing, and chairs would be provided.*

Joan Whitehead: *They used to come out specially to watch T.V.* (at the Britannia in 1951). *We were the first in Nunnery Lane to have one, it was a big attraction. Now they come out to get away from it.*

Don Nixon: *My elder brother took it over* (Mr. Nixon's elder brother Alan, took over the licence of the Golden Lion from his parents in 1955). *He transformed that room,* (the upstairs meeting room) *because he was the first publican in York to have a colour television. And everybody, but everybody, wanted to be upstairs.*

67. The Britannia Inn, Nunnery Lane, in the early part of the century.

(York Oral History Society)

So much so that he put a little cocktail bar in the corner. It hit the national papers that one, about the first public house to have a colour television.

Sheila White: *I had a piano player on a Friday, Saturday and Sunday night* (at the Jubilee in the 1960s). *You had different ones get up and sing, they think that they're stars. They liked entertaining, we didn't have any television. When you started off in the '60s, televisions weren't a pub thing. It was jukeboxes and live music on a weekend. The pubs in town in the 60s, they all had jukeboxes and it was the turn of music really – the Beatles era and all that business, putting their money into jukeboxes and dancing about.*

Arthur Briggs: *In 1953 I got a T.V. put in, that was Coronation year. It was the first T.V. round here. There was a Coronation party on that day, and it rained, and we let all the kids come in, 'cos they'd never seen a television. I got a jukebox in. I got 'Radio Relay' in first, then I put a record player in as well – Ray Conniff, Jim Reeves, nice background. When this new, modern stuff came in, I used to get cassettes. I relayed it all through the pub.*

Bob Barker: *Saturday nights we used to have sing songs, there were some lovely singers among 'em. We got an R.A.F. (group) the 'Trailblazers' they called 'em,*

68. The 'Trailblazers' who provided regular entertainment at the Brown Cown in the late 1960s. *(Bob Barker)*

they were actually stationed at Linton-on-Ouse in the later years. They were country and western, played on a Saturday night. They didn't want any money, as long as they got a few beers.

Joan Whitehead: *Jazz was up and running* (at the Spotted Cow) *in 1957 or '58, we were the first pub that started it – Wednesday, Friday, and Sunday, oh, we had some wonderful nights. We got very full, sitting on the stairs, I'll bet over 100 – 130, 140 – you know what jazz is like, the more packed, the more they like it. They'd be sitting at a table and the band's there right on top of them, it was a wonderful atmosphere – Duke Ellington, that kind of stuff, Ella Fitzgerald. Tunes that everybody knew. I got up one night and said, "Can I sing so-and-so?" – what ever song it was –" With you?" And they said, "Yeah" and ever after that, "Are you going to give us a song?". I couldn't always get up if we were real busy, but I'd give them a couple of turns after eleven o'clock. I used to book some professionals, but not very often. Do you know Digby Fairweather? He's been with Fred Hunt. Digby on trumpet and Fred on piano. I used to charge a couple of pounds. They'd probably be doing a gig over in Leeds, and so they used to stop with me, and I'd pay them the money that we'd taken at the door, and they were quite happy.*

Barbara Fletcher: *It seemed to be in the sixties when groups started in pubs. We had a piano and drums to start with, and then we started with groups – practically from when we went in* (to the Londesbro' Hotel in 1961). *We went to all the pubs that had groups in, to find out which was the best group. Listen to 'em and try to book 'em, and get into trouble! – 'pinchin' my group' sort of thing. Molly from the 'Burns' was a stickler. She used to say, "You're not coming in to listen to my group tonight, 'cos you'll want 'em". But we did have some, and it was really nice. We had a live group in maybe Monday, Wednesday and every Saturday. You paid twenty, twenty five pound in them days, you couldn't get a group for under that. So you had to take a lot of money, but they used to queue to come in, and I mean queue. We had Gerry B and the Rockefellars. Dustin Gee used to wear my clothes you know, he used to say, "Leave me a pair of corsets out, and your bras", and he used to get dressed up in my clothes. He was one of the best, was Dustin Gee. One night Freddie and the Dreamers were playing at the Theatre Royal, with the Mindbenders. And we knew the manager, so he said, "Oh, we'll bring Freddie and the Dreamers down". Anyway, they came . . . it was gone eleven when we'd finished. I got the lounge cleared up, and then we let Freddie and the Dreamers and the Mindbenders in the back way. They never played, it was supposed to be a little friendly, but the crowds got to know about it, and the police came, and shouted, "Everybody out". And Freddie ran upstairs when he saw the police coming and headed into a room. They all had to go home. And it was the first and only time I had to go to the police court on a Saturday morning, with my head in my hands and say,"I'm sorry". That was a good night, but I got into trouble for it.*

69. The Londesbro' Arms, Petergate (middle left of picture). 1970s. *(City of York Archives)*

8. THE SECOND WORLD WAR

The Second World War was a time of danger and excitement, when everyone was determined to use their free time to live life to the full, to enjoy themselves, to make the most of each moment. This applied to those involved on the home front as well as the servicemen fighting the war: 'Drink and be merry, for tomorrow . . . ?' York was the place where many allied airmen from Europe and the Commonwealth came to make the most of the time they had between 'ops'. So, of course, the city pubs were lively, pulsating places, packed to the doors – when beer was available.

Joan Whitehead: *There was a feeling that we've never had since. The cameraderie. Everybody was friends, everybody helped each other, it was fantastic. It's hard to explain, but it was a wonderful time really, for young people.*

Eric Shaw: *During t'war , when I was in bed on t'top floor, and with all the racket going on down below, they never heard t'sirens. So I used to to get out of bed, come down this passageway, poke me head through t'wall and shout down that siren's goin'. And of course they'd cry,"Oh siren's goin'". Nobody bothered, they still kept drinkin'. And that was it. One night they dropped a bomb on t'gasworks in Monkgate, and it shattered. There was a tailor's shop opposite the Angler's Arms, and it simply shattered that window, all caved in. And that stopped 'em singin' and dancin' for a bit, and drinkin'. But they went back to it again. They all went outside and had a look and came back in again.*

Doreen Bolton: *You got lads in, they were all airforce, all fliers. I think they just lived for today, for tomorrow we may die. I had Australians and Canadians. It was false, you didn't know whether you were going to live or not, did yer really? You was just sort of happy.*

Pauline Worthy: *A lot of hustle and bustle, a lot of singin', there were lots of dances, a lot of happy people. We all had a really good time, 'cos tomorrow we don't know where we would be. Me dad used to put on a meal at Christmas for an aircrew. The living room, the kitchen was all turned over to them, so they could all have a meal in a home, I guess.*

Sheila White: *First time I went in a pub was with a Canadian friend of mine, and that was the White Swan (in Piccadilly) and they had a band, four piece band. It was very nice, very busy, loads of people in, and all nationalities: French, Canadian, Polish, American – although the Americans didn't come at first, they came at the end. There were always plenty of people about, well, you couldn't get in. It's like Saturday nights now in pubs in town.*

Doreen Greaves: *She had a big safe (her mother at the Pack Horse) and she had pint pots inside, and they all (aircrews) used to put their money in, and they used*

70. Doreen Bolton and Meg Heatley enjoy a night out with unknown escort. 1940s.
(Pauline Worthy)

to say to my mother, "If I buy it tomorrow night, that's for so-and-so to have a good drink". That's the way it used to be. I've seen twelve pots in there.

Joan Whitehead: *These Canadians, all seven of them, from the pilot down, they'd leave something behind the bar* (at the Three Tuns). *"Mrs. Farrington, will you put that behind the bar, that's our lucky charm". Didn't always work though.*

Returning home on leave, some of the Phoenix customers found its attraction irresistible, and didn't want to go back to their stations . . .

Lily Grayson: *In war time when they were on leave, and they'd overstayed their leave, the redcaps used to come for 'em – they allus knew where to look. They used to shoot out of the bar, climb over the wall and on to the moat, and off they used to go – they used to run away, but eventually they were caught.*

A time of anxiety, pent-up emotion and hard drinking, coupled with a loss of peace-time morality and family restraint, and often being a long way from home, meant that trouble was not only found in the skies, or at the 'front'.

Doreen Bolton: *French-Canadians were the only ones I had any trouble with, starting to fight. It frightened me one night, I had them barred from the pub altogether.*

Doreen Greaves: *Occasionally young airmen would say to me mother, "Can I take her to the Co-op dance?" and I used to go there, and they used to escort me home. I once walked in with a lad one night and there was the most awful fight going on between the Free French and the French-Canadians. Anyway I got out all right, but there were knives and all sorts whizzing about. That's why they called it* (the Co-op dance hall), *'Buckets of blood'. I remember one night at the Pack Horse and these Canadians came in, and they all trooped out when we called time, and they left one behind, and he was an Indian, a Red Indian. Oh he was a big broad feller, and he had a chip on his shoulder – nobody would talk to him in England – and I could see my mother talking to him, trying to calm him down. And I climbed over the counter and dropped down into the front bar, and I flew into Micklegate and I stopped two Canadian redcaps* (military policemen). *They came inside with me, and I could see the relief on my mother's face. She was still talking to him, and he said, "Nobody's offered me a meal, just because I'm a Red Indian". And she said, "Well love, you can come to me for a meal anytime, but you'll have to go now, it's closing time", and these military policemen didn't do a thing. Anyway, she got him outside and slammed the door after him, and she said, "I hope to God he doesn't remember where he was. If he comes back he'll murder me". But that was the only time I saw my Mother frightened. I wouldn't say they were particularly fight-conscious.*

Pauline Worthy: *We only had one lot of trouble, when somebody stabbed somebody in our men's urinals. There wasn't a death, but somebody just stuck a knife in his stomach, I think. I think they were Canadians.* (In May 1944 the Yorkshire Evening Press reported that an R.A.F. Sergeant had been fined £20 for stabbing a Canadian airman in the stomach at the Talbot Hotel, in a fight over a girl.) *That's the only thing I can remember, but there was a lot of argy-bargy after the pubs turned out, a lot of slanging. I was always keen to be hanging out of the window watchin' what went on. That was great excitement.*

Drink was rationed, and pubs often ran out of beer. This resulted in many publicans closing their doors during official opening hours, leading to complaints from members of the public. Landlords were split on the action to be taken, and one landlord wrote, in a letter to the Yorkshire Evening Press in August 1945, that, 'even if a pub has no beer it should still remain open. For a pub should be a club, and not merely a place for drinking'. Eventually the York Licensing Justices decided that licensed premises in the City must remain open certain minimum hours daily, the minimum periods being 12 – 2p.m. and 8 – 10p.m. on Sundays, and 12 – 2p.m and 5.30 – 9p.m. on weekdays. Publicans often tried to obtain alcohol from 'other sources', and the pub was sometimes a place where black-market items could be obtained.

Pauline Worthy: *You had contacts during the war, and if anybody had any meat or eggs or butter, me dad saw that we got some of it. You got the farmers in*

71. The City Arms, Fawcett Street in 1952. The City Arms was one of the hotels run by the Morris family, well known York hoteliers. Others included the White Swan, Piccadilly, and the Chase, Tadcaster Road. *(City of York Archives)*

Parliament Street on a Saturday, and they'd come in the pub, or go in the Clock, Bill Hesp's pub. And if you had the money you could get the goods. And me dad had the money. We did run out of beer from time to time, you had an allocation. But if we ran out of spirits we used to ring up, say, Solly Morris at the White Swan in Piccadilly. I know me dad's been to the White Swan to pick up spirits because we've run out. If you lent it to others, they paid you back when their allocation came in.

Sheila White: *And then it was rationed, and if a pub got some beer, then everybody knew about it. They used to run and line up to get in, but they didn't get a full supply. And of course your little local pubs, they had their regulars, and they didn't like to serve other people. You could only get beer, if anybody had any spirits they used to keep them for their regular customers. If you went into a smart hotel there used to be Pimms, Pimms I, 2, and 3, – gin, whisky and rum based. They were very expensive, they were five shillings – that was in your Station Hotel and your White Swan, and possibly the Chase.*

Doreen Bolton: *I'd maybe open on a Thursday night, then you keep 'em guessin', maybe not open 'til Saturday night, and I always liked to open on a Sunday might if I could – you didn't know what to do to be right. We used to fiddle around a bit, I don't know if you'd call it black-market or not. I used to get some stuff off Walker and Scotts, 'cos I knew a feller who had that, but that was all spirits though. I've had what you call an 'eighteen' of beer* (an eighteen gallon barrel of beer), *that Solly* (Solly Morris from the White Swan Hotel) *used to let me have, in the back of an ice-cream van. Canadian lads were good, they'd get me bottles of whisky, they used to bring cigs to me, 'Sweet Cap' they used to call 'em. And of course we used to do black-market with grub. Strensall . . . it was small time convicts who'd been put in the Army, and they used to bring suitcases full, meat and tea. And they used to take it in t'snug, and of course all customers used to be queueing up. Oh God! what a carry on! They used to fire-watch at Wright's Pork Butchers, and I used to go across, and there'd be chops and steak and sausages. We used to have a right tuck in. And I gave 'em a feather bed to sleep on – they wasn't supposed to, but they did! But you were happy, it was a good laugh. Seth Aspinall was a real character, he was a rugby player and a butcher, and he had a bike that they used to deliver meat on. He came in one day, and he flew upstairs, and he dashed downstairs, and next thing two 'tecs came in* (detectives) *and they said to Seth, "Where's your bike?" So Seth says, "It's out the back". He'd run upstairs and put a pig in our bedroom, in my bed! Bloody pig in bed! Ooh they used to do some things, honestly.*

John Greaves: *Me mother used to get food where she could, for the transport drivers, that sort of thing. She used to get farmers coming in that had a bit on the side. It had to be done to keep the place going. Somebody sent her a pig, a pig in* *a poke, a live one, you know, it was won in a raffle or something. And she says, "No, I don't want it, you're breaking the law". So she got a taxi, and was going to send it back to Bubwith. And this damn pig was sat in the back of the taxi, looking out of the window. She didn't want to go to prison . . . for a pig.*

The overwhelming desire to 'have a good time' in a dangerous age meant that, in the Second World War, not only were the pubs overflowing, but so too were the dance halls – and the De Grey Rooms was one of the places to be.

72. Bert Keech, third from left, with members of his band at the De Grey Rooms, which at this time – in the 1940s – included Geoff Love senior (kneeling at the front).

(Edith Keech)

9. FOOD – GLORIOUS FOOD?

Before the outbreak of the Second World War the local pub was the place where people went to drink, have a sing-song, a game of darts, and to talk about the issues of the day. They didn't go there to eat, except on special occasions: pub outings, dart matches, annual dinners, funerals, weddings, and the like. The places that catered for food were usually the larger, well-ordered premises and hotels, usually on the main routes through the city, where travellers from the West Riding, going to or from the east coast resorts, could break their journey, although some 'locals' would serve meals for regular business men customers. With post war prosperity and a great rise in car ownership, and women working in large numbers and wanting to spend less time at the kitchen sink, the need to provide meals in a greater variety and number of licensed premises became apparent. By the 1960s many local and country inns, where the humble crisp had formerly been the only source of sustenance, were experimenting with chicken and scampi in a basket, and other such culinary delights.

Lily Grayson: *No there was no food, not even sandwiches* (at the Phoenix in the 1930s and '40s). *Me dad used to say, "You get food in a cafe, you get beer in a pub".*

Mabel Wilson: *There wasn't catering like there is now* (during the 1910s and '20s). *There wasn't facilities to do catering. On Carlin Sunday – that's the Sunday before Easter – you used to have carlins, they were like mushy peas, but they were brown. And the landlord also gave them on Boxing Day and drinks all round, and sandwiches and things, so you were always packed. We used to have charabanc rides, men and women separately, take them to the seaside. But they were open and if you got on Whitby moors and it came on to rain, you were drenched before you got the thing* (hood) *pulled over. But they used to get breakfast, dinner and tea, one or two of those a year, on a Sunday.*

Noel Attree: *Me grandma* (Mrs. Davison at the Red Lion) *used to put on a little meal at lunch-time for one or two, you know. Stubbs, the ironmonger people. On the opposite side of the road was a feller called Bob Whitehead, he was a big taxi business, he used to come in. Old Mr. Ellerker, where Ellerker's shop was, he'd maybe call in. There was always a little meal and a drink.*

Eric Shaw: *He had a big glass dish on the counter* (his father at the Angler's Arms), *with a knob on, and that was full of crisps, and that was about the only food, maybe a few cheese biscuits, that was about all. There was one bloke who came round Friday and Saturday night, he'd have his white smock on, he was spotless, with a big basket. And it was full of mussels, winkles, prawns, and stuff like that. Thre'pence a packet, summat like that in them days.*

73. A charabanc trip from the Red Lion, Merchantgate, ready to depart sometime in the 1920s. John Davison, son of licensee Christina, is sitting on the running board holding a trilby.

(Michael Hannay)

Pauline Worthy: *Crisps were about as much as you could get, Smith's Crisps. But there were occasions when my dad and mam would put things on for customers, like Carlin Sunday, me dad would put on Carlin peas. They're like black peas, and he used to take it round to customers in little dishes.*

Pauline Coldrick: *Crisps, potato crisps, that's all* (at the Frog Hall). *We had pickled eggs, always sandwiches on darts night, but not food for sale as such. I hear from old aunties that it was always a tradition on a Sunday night for the landlord to make sandwiches and put them on the bar for the customers, and that certainly happened at the Waggon and Horses* (in Gillygate). *That would be just before the war.*

Edith Keech: *They were lovely, all the customers there* (at the Minster Inn). *We used to have suppers occasionally – special nights.*

Sheila White: *The Jubilee was very good, very nice people, and they drank well. They've only small houses, so I did all the catering for them. There was never a weekend I didn't have a wedding, or a 21st, 18th, and even unfortunately when people died, I used to do funeral teas for them. The Jubilee was the hub of Leeman*

74. Staff, family and customers - including some dedicated followers of fashion - outside the Minster Inn prior to a pub supper. c.1970.   *(Edith Keech)*

75. The Jubilee Hotel, Balfour Street. c.1970.   *(Sheila White)*

Road. I used to employ six ladies off Leeman Road, they were waitresses, and I did all the cooking and catering. And when it was darts night I used to put roast potatoes in the oven, hot sausage rolls and make sandwiches, pickles. On a Sunday I used to put cheese and biscuits and pickles on the bar for people to eat. It was good.

John Greaves: *From the early days they used to get parties coming along* (at the Lion and Lamb in the 1920s and '30s), *then the transport drivers arrived on the scene. She* (his mother) *was the founder of what they called the 'Bedford Driver's Club'. So she was always into the catering side, she did a lot of catering, 'cos there wasn't so much around in those days. She developed a big staff, people coming in. I heard her say she once had a thousand meals in a weekend. She didn't serve meals as they do today, just catered for parties. There wasn't even sandwiches knocking about in those days . . . crisps and biscuits.*

Doreen Greaves: *In fact when they introduced crisps – round about the '20s – you used to get big tins of Smith's Crisps, and they asked John's dad to be the agent for York, for them. And he said to Mary* (Mrs. Greaves), *"What do you think about these crisps Mary?" He was all for it, but she pooh-poohed the idea, so they never got 'em. She once, when she used to do evening dinners, she says,"Go and ask 'em what they want to start with". So I says to this gentleman, "What do you want, halibut or soup?" She used to give 'em a full halibut steak for starter! So he says, "What's halibut?" I says, "You're having soup!"*

Joan Whitehead: *In those days* (the early 1950s at the Britannia Inn), *all the coaches from Leeds going to Scarborough used to come down Nunnery Lane. And we used to do a lot of breakfasts for the coach trade, and then get 'em back at night time to drink. And when it was the races, Norman, my husband, used to write on the window: 'Ham and Egg Lunches, 2/6', and when they'd gone to the races, he would change it to 'Ham and Egg Teas, 2/6'. And then in March '54 we went to the Spotted Cow, we'd two market days a week, wonderful days, 'cos they were packed all the time. We used to do market lunches. It wasn't a la carte: Soup or Yorkshire pudding as a first course. Roast beef or lamb or pork. Used to make me own steak pies. And a sweet and a coffee. Forget how much it was, 4/6 or something.*

Lela Norfolk: *We might have a bus in, and they'd let you know, see if you'll put some sandwiches on. You could never get more than a packet of crisps in a pub, you know, no food like there is now. I'll tell you what I started with* (around 1960): *pies and peas, little pork pies. I used to warm 'em up, and soak loads of peas, you know. It was tasty, they liked 'em.*

Barbara Fletcher: *When we did away with groups we started cooking. I was in the Daily Mirror loads of times for good food.* (We did) *everything that you would see on a bar lunch – scampi, fish, pies, curries.*

76. Pub trips were very popular both prior to and after the Second World War, before the time when most people had a car. Here a group from the Minster Inn in the 1920s ('hats off for the camera gentlemen') are ready for a day out. *(Edith Keech)*

Ron Powell: *They did catering for parties, that is association, works . . . a lot West Riding and even Lancashire people. They used to get up at six, and they would be going to Whitby or Scarborough. First stop was York, and they wanted gammon slices with two eggs and some mushrooms, and others had tomatoes – whatever they wanted, they could have. They would always let you know beforehand. And they could have three coaches on a Sunday morning, one after the other. Midday meals were rare, very rare, they had a long way to go and were back in York for about five. Sometimes they has cooked fish for tea, with potatoes and parsley sauce, sometimes a salad with cold ham. Breakfast used to cost two shillings to half a crown, teas could be a similar price, and if they had fresh fruit – which was called fresh fruit even though it wasn't – it came out of a bottle with a glass top with a rubber washer – and that could cost as much as three shillings.*

SUMMER MENUS.		DINNER MENUS.	
BREAKFASTS:		No. 1 Menu at 2/6 per Head.	
Fillets of Fish, Ham and Eggs. Scones, Bread and Butter, Jam or Marmalade, Tea and Coffee.	2 6 per Head.	SOUP—Oxtail. JOINTS—Roast Lamb and Mint Sauce. Roast Beef, Yorkshire Pudding. Vegetables in season. SWEET—Fruit Tart, Biscuits and Cheese.	
Ham and Eggs, Scones Bread and Butter, Jam or Marmalade Tea and Coffee.	2/- per Head.		
COLD LUNCHEON:		No. 2 Menu at 3/- per Head.	
Soup, Cold Boiled Salmon, Cucumber Mayonnaise, Cold Lamb Mint Sauce, Cold Beef, Vegetables, Salads, Fruit Tart and Custard, Biscuits and Cheese.	3 6 per Head.	SOUP—Tomato or Oxtail. FISH—Cod and Shrimp Sauce. JOINTS—Roast Lamb, Yorkshire Pudding. Mint Sauce, Roast Beef. Vegetables in season. SWEET—Fruit Tart and Custard. Biscuits and Cheese.	
TEAS:			
Salmon Mayonnaise, Cold Chicken and Ham, Fruit and Custard, Bread and Butter, Pastries.	3/6 per Head.	No. 3 Menu at 3/6 per Head.	
Hot Filleted Fish, Cold Ham and Tongue, Salads, Bread and Butter, Pastries.	2/6 per Head.	SOUP—Oxtail or Tomato. FISH—Turbot and Shrimp Sauce. ENTREE—Cutlets, Madras Sauce. JOINTS—Roast Beef. Roast Lamb and Mint Sauce. Vegetables in season.	
Cold Ham and Tongue or Beef, Salads, Bread and Butter, Pastries.	2/3 per Head.	SWEET—Fruit Tart, Compote of Fruit and Custard. Biscuits and Cheese.	

77. The menu from the Bay Horse, Blossom Street. 1930s. *(Ron Powell)*

Bob Barker: *We always did pie and peas for dart matches . . . roast taties sometime. We bought an infra red machine, before microwaves came out, this was about 1970. You could make a bacon sandwich, you put it in this special . . . like polythene, and you just put it in this machine, and it had a blue light, infra red, and it used to cook the bread and bacon.*

Sometimes those with a delicate constitution could be put off their food.

Doug Dalton: *I'll never forget one Saturday morning, father had just got these pork pies, and these two old dears came in, and he'd just started cutting these pork pies, putting some sauce and stuff on, with half a pint, whatever it was they were drinkin'. And we had this great big tabby cat, Fluff we called her. She comes out of the staircase with this damned great mouse in her mouth, sits down in front of 'em, and just starts crunchin' this mouse. These old dears just looked at this mouse, looked at the pork pies, put their knives down and walked out.*

10. 'MINE'S A?' WHAT DRINKERS DRANK

Beer has been the main drink quaffed in the English pub for hundreds of years. The traditional drink of the working man in this century was draught mild or bitter. But times and people change, and by the 1960s pub customers were more widely travelled, open to experiment and receptive (some might say highly susceptible!) to advertising. With the brewers producing a variety of drinks to satisfy most palates, mild beer lost its popularity, and beers previously foreign to the English palate took its place – including lager, which accounted for only two per cent of all beer sales in 1959; by 1989 it accounted for fifty per cent. The large numbers of women coming into pubs also meant a greater variety of drinks needed to be stocked – the request for, 'a pint for me and a half for the wife' was beginning to be a thing of the past.

Eric Shaw: *Mild and bitter really, on draught, out of barrels, but bitter mainly* (the main drinks at the Angler's Arms in the 1930s). *Occasionally you'd get a bloke coming in asking for a pint of mixed. You'd never see a woman with a pint. If she was going to drink beer she'd either be drinkin' Magnet, which was always served in a fancy glass, or she'd have half of bitter. If she wasn't drinkin' beer, she'd be on milk stout. Very rare did you see 'em drinkin' 'gin and it'.*

Noel Attree: *Mostly, it was bitter, a pint of bitter* (at the Red Lion in the 1920s/30s). *John Smith's dark mild – when you lifted it up to the light, it was just like a port wine colour, real deep, with a good head on it. Guinness sold well. Guinness used to have a cork in it, and you used to have a contraption, it was made of brass, and it was screwed into the top of the counter, and there was a winding handle on it, and you put your bottle on the bottom end, wind this thing*

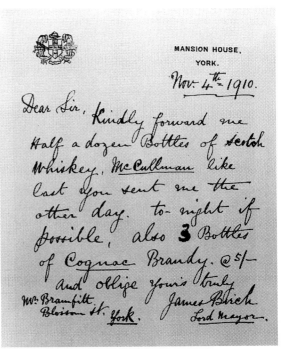

MANSION HOUSE,
YORK.

Nov. 4th 1910.

Dear Sir,
Kindly forward me Half a dozen Bottles of Scotch Whiskey, McCullman like last you sent me the other day. to-night if possible, also 3 Bottles of Cognac Brandy. @ 5/– And oblige yours truly
Mr. Bramfitt
Blossom St. York.
James Birch
Lord Mayor.

78. An urgent order from the Lord Mayor to the landlord of the Lion and Lamb! *(John Greaves)*

79. The Woolpack, Fawcett Street, 1930s.   *(York Oral History Society)*

towards you, and the spile went in, and you pulled it the other way, and you pulled the cork out. Women, old ones, drank a bottle of Guinness or a bottle of Bass. We used to sell shorts, rum and pep. I often used to go for a bottle of peppermint to Melrose's, opposite W.P. Brown's. There was a lovely counter, all polished wood, very Dickensian. What you wanted was all written down beautifully, in longhand. Jimmy Melrose used to sit outside sellimg yeast – lived to be 100.

My mother had a wonderful little bar (at the Woolpack in Fawcett Street in the 1930s), *she always had a wonderful variety of drinks, far better than the Red Lion. You could have Grand Marnier, Creme De Menthe, Angostura Bitters, anything you wanted. In those days the Rialto was on the go, and more often than not, the people who were appearing on those shows used to call in.*

Mabel Wilson: *Port and lemon was a ladies' drink in those days, you were very exciting if you had a port and lemon.*

Fred Veitch: *In those days there was a lot of mild sold. I can remember the prices during the war; mild was 4d a pint, bitter was 6d, so the majority of the working class people drank mild because it was cheaper. I never drank mild in me life, because I used to see what happened to it. All the slops went into a trough and all* *that went into the barrels, and they always went into the mild, 'cos bitter had to settle and you couldn't disturb it once you'd started on it. A lot of women drank stout, some women used to drink port and lemon. Very few spirits were sold – a solicitor used to come in and drink whisky. I shouldn't imagine we sold a bottle of whisky a month.*

Stan Leaf: *There weren't a lot of lager drinkers* (in the Phoenix in 1963). *It was mostly bitter – and dark mild, we used to sell a lot of dark mild. Dark mild was one and three a pint, bitter one and five – one and six.*

Ron Powell: *It was always beer and porter . . . stout as well. They*

80. Landlord Reg Leaf and his wife Gladys in the doorway of the Phoenix, George Street. c.1960.
(Gladys Leaf)

also had Magnet Old, which was a very strong beer, close to barley wine. That fell off, because it was a specialist beer, and in its place was a nine gallon Magnet Ale, that was always straight from the wood. Port and lemon, that was the ladies' drink – a measure of port and filled up nearly to half a pint with lemonade.

Doreen Bolton: *Bitter, light mild, and dark mild, but I only used to serve dark mild. A lot of publicans used to serve light mild for bitter – if they could get away with it. I used to sell pints of bitter for sixpence. Ladies used to drink beer . . . some Guinness, and if they were well off, they'd have a drop of short. They used to have baby Guinness then. Guinness was only seven pence a bottle, and baby Guinness was four pence. You could charge extra in your smoke-room, you'd get a better . . . if a feller came in with his lady friend, he'd tek' her in t'smoke-room, he wouldn't take her in t'bar. Tetley's was always a good beer, they used to say a pint of Hunt's kept the toilet clean. But it's an acquired taste, like everything else.*

Barbara Fletcher: *For men it was beer, just beer, beer, beer – bitter.*

Pauline Worthy: *Pints of mild, pints of bitter, Guinness, black and tans. The women? Half of milds, things like that. The working men drank their pints, the business people drank their halves. As I remember it anyhow.*

81. A new beer, 'Celebration Ale' is delivered to the Londesbro' Arms in 1971. Mrs Fletcher, centre; daughter Jean, on her right, and husband Jim, arms outstretched, ceremoniously collect the first delivery. *(Barbara Fletcher)*

Don Nixon: *Always had mild in those days* (in the 1950s at the Golden Lion). *If you had any beer to put back it always went into the mild – it's all right people saying mild was the dumping ground for other beers, but it enhanced it, it didn't degrade it.*

But the times, 'they were a-changing', and by the 1960s variety was the spice of life.

Don Nixon: *I think there's no explanation for it* (why mild beer stopped being drunk). *I think that lighter beers . . . people used to drink with their eyes, if one person lifted a pint and looked through it, everybody did. Another stepping stone was the introduction of lager, when we talk about mild drinkers, they're probably the lager drinkers we have now. Didn't like bitter beer, enjoyed the mild beer, and now gone on to lager.*

Pauline Coldrick: *The youngsters, the lads, when they started bringing their girls in* (to the Frog Hall in the 1960s), *then they'd have these . . . was it Snake Bites? Was that lager and cider? Funny sort of things. And of course Babychams and*

117

those sort of things came in, but married women stuck to the beer, or Guinness, or whatever they drank. They didn't change their drinks at all.

Arthur Briggs: *When lager came in, the first I got was 'Harp'. I never thought it would go, but now there's more supped than anything.*

Eve Briggs: *In 1953, '54, you could sell cases and cases of Babycham. It was one and thre'pence, and you got it in a proper glass, with a cherry. We used to sell quite a lot of bottled beers, Magnet, milk stout, but nobody buys 'em now. I used to make my own drinks and flame 'em, you know, set fire to 'em, winter nights. 'Eve's Specials'; brandy . . . Angostura Bitters . . . sugar round edge of t'glass . . . brandy flavours. I used to burn ends of me fingers flaming 'em. People used to be fascinated. I never even told my barmaid how to make 'em. You had to have your own gimmicks, you see.*

Betty Harris: *It was mild, it was bitter,* (at the Golden Lion, St. Sampson's Square), *and something people used to drink then was a pint of mixed, half of mild and half of bitter, it was hugely popular. And as far as I remember nobody had mixes, certainly you never heard of anybody having a gin and tonic; there was orange, there was blackcurrant, there was lime, there was peppermint – rum and pep. But it was peppermint cordial. When we took the Woodman, mild would be eleven pence a pint, and bitter one and a penny. That was in 1960. By the '60s*

82. Behind the bar of the Mount Hotel, circa 1960. From the size of the containers on the bar it would appear that 'Occo Crush' was a big seller! *(Lela Norfolk)*

there was a huge difference in women's drinks, there were women coming into the pub all the time, young women. There was Babycham, there was Pony – huge sellers. There was a drink called Orangillo, all those little bottle things. Huge change in drinking habits, but mainly because women were coming in. It had been a man's domain, he'd bring his wife on a Saturday night; gin and orange, but no more than that. The breweries could see that this was going to be a huge market, and it was.

Vera Lyall: *The main change was when lager started, and you got more varieties of drink for women. In my day it was gin and orange, which was vile anyway, then people started going abroad, and they came back with these ideas for drinks, and you had to get in touch. 'Snowball' was the big thing, from about '68, I should imagine. They were a blooming nuisance, used to take you ages to do, and you couldn't use the glasses again. You had to wash them separately, they were all sticky. Them and that Cyprus drink – smelt of aniseed – Pernod. You couldn't do them in the normal manner, like you do with beer glasses.*

John Greaves: *Pre-war and just after the war we would be doing about thirteen to fourteen barrels* (selling 36 gallon barrels of beer a week) *and it didn't vary a lot. And then when they altered the pub, the actual volume of real ale dropped. The youngsters were going on to Double Diamond – the keg stuff, and lager, and the young girls were drinkin' soft drinks. So the real ale dropped, but the actual barrelage increased. In the late '60s we used to sell six barrels of Double Diamond a week, that's thirty six gallon barrels. I remember a director saying to me," You're doing very well. Do you realise you're doing 16 barrels a week?"*

Bob Barker: *I used to wait on at the Grey Mare* (Clifton) *in the 1950s. There the whisky used to come in a barrel, and it had to be watered down. The whisky was 100% proof, and you had to put so many grammes of water in it, and the Customs and Excise used to come and test it. They didn't have optics then, you had a little pewter pot, you had a measure in. They used to sell what they called barley wine – I mean you get barley wine in bottles, but it wasn't the same – it was in a gallon barrel on the counter with a tap. And you turned the tap on and it came out like molasses, and they always supplied a wooden, long bladed, palette knife, and when you turned the tap off you cut it, you know. Then you just put a drop of beer in, it was really potent.*

Sheila White: *Snakebites, it's lager and cider, that was fashionable in the '70s. Some wise guy found out that if you drank half a pint of lager and half a pint of cider together it was stingo – the lights went out!*

Young people becoming drunk, ill, and stupid after buying new, unfamiliar drinks that taste like fruit juices, but which have a high alcohol content, is not a new phenomenon.

83. Mr. Sandland, the landlord, stands outside the Old Grey Mare, Clifton, in 1936. Mr. Sandland was a well known pre-war licensee. Between 1907 and 1938 he held, consecutively, the tenancies of the Admiral Hawke, Walmgate; The Victoria Inn, Heslington Road; and the Old Grey Mare. *(Mike Prime)*

Sheila White: *They used to sell some little bottles of things, 'Johnny Pine'. It tasted like pineapple, but that was a rocket. And there was another thing, 'Cherry B'. 'Cherry B' and 'Pine' – you think pineapples and cherries, but sickly, nasty things they were. But the kids used to buy them. That was in the '60s.*

On one occasion over indulgence of one of these drinks led to tragedy:

Doug Dalton: *When I was there* (at the Greyhound, Spurriergate) *they brought out this thing, Pino. It was very potent, it was pineapple spiked with something. It was actually quite a nice drink, but it caused the death of one York girl. A lad over-indulged on the stuff one night, and he ended up strangling her. It came out that he'd been in our pub buying this Pino. When the court case was on, and he was up for trial, just about everybody from court came and tried this Pino. We couldn't get enough of it.*

Sometimes a request for the 'exotic' could cause confusion:

Bob Barker: *I always remember I was down in the cellar, and this motor cyclist came in with t'helmet, he took it off, stood at the bar, "I'll have a screw driver".* *She* (his wife who was serving behind the bar at the Brown Cow) *shouted down,*

"Where's your screw driver?" I came up and said, "Here you are, why?" She said, "He's asked for one". I said, "Yes, that's . . . " – you know! (A 'screwdriver' drink is a cocktail of vodka and orange juice). *We had a big Irishman, worked at power stations, and the first time he came in, he said, "Would it be possible to have a doctor?" I said, "You mean a drink?" He said, "Yes, I don't mean a . . . you know". So I said, "What is it?" And he said, "A meaure of this . . . a measure of that". He had rum, vodka, whisky, gin, brandy, in a pint glass, then he'd say, "I want a half pint in there". And he came in every Saturday!*

Although running a pub wasn't all 'beer and skittles', for all life was there – and trouble and tragedy will go hand in hand with laughter and joy – most publicans found it a rich and rewarding life:

Joan Whitehead: *Many times we didn't even have a night off, we just stopped in the pub and played darts with the lads. It was more a friendly, homely atmosphere. All your customers were friends. All my life I've had pleasant memories, I've had fun, I've really enjoyed it. If I went tomorrow, I've no regrets. My husband was the same, he loved the licensed trade. He didn't have hobbies – his work was his hobby.*

84. Joan and Norman Whitehead behind the well stocked bar at the Spotted Cow Hotel. 1970s.   *(Joan Whitehead)*

SUMMARY

The stories in this book are just snippets taken from hours of conversations, and in the case of some of the interviewees, over more than one visit to their homes. I feel privileged to have gained a glimpse into their lives, to see a world that has faded, almost slipped away, that exists in very few places. Attempts by modern pub designers to recreate the past seem to produce sterile premises that are facsimiles, rather than flourishing reflections of it. Only continuity of use of actual fixtures and fittings, and memories passed from generation to generation, can hope to truly retain a feel for 'what it was like then'. I hope the memories contained within these pages have thrown a chink of light through that closed curtain. I hope you have smelled the beer, tasted the crisps, heard the laughter, and felt the past come again, briefly, alive!

BIBLIOGRAPHY

Benson, G. *The Taverns, Hostels, and Inns of York* (Booklet)

Bradley, T. *The Old Coaching Days in Yorkshire* Yorkshire Conservative Newspaper Co.

Cooper, T.P. *The Old Inns and Inn Signs of York* Delittle & Fenwick.

Hackwood, F.W. *Inns, Ales, and Drinking Customs of Old England* Bracken Books.

Haydon, P. *The English Pub: A History* Robert Hale.

Hutt, C. *The Death of the English Pub* Arrow.

Kay, R. *Grandfather Robert Kay's Book 1875-1900 (Diary observing life in Walmgate)*

Licensed Victuallers Association minute books 1910-1948.

Miles, J.G. *Innkeeping. A Manual for Licensed Victuallers* Brewing Publications Ltd.

Taylor, A.R. *Pub Games* Mayflower.

Williams, G.P. and Brake, G.T. *The English Public House in Transition* Edsall.

York Historian, Volume 10 Yorkshire Architectural and York Archeological Society. 1991.

Yorkshire Courant 1789.

Yorkshire Evening Press 1923, 1944-5, 1960.

Yorkshire Gazette 1834, 1846, 1848, 1924.

Yorkshire Herald 1903, 1912, 1914.

ABOUT THE AUTHOR

Mike Race was born in York and spent most of his working life in the printing trade, mainly at Rowntrees. Always interested in history – national, local and family – he is currently chairman of the York Oral History Society, and also enjoys gardening, reading, sport in general, watching York City in particular, and going for the 'odd pint' with family and friends. His interest in pubs stems from a long family involvement in the trade, going back to mid-Victorian times, but he admits, with some shame, to be one of the few members from the paternal side of his family who have never 'pulled a pint'. Mike is married with two daughters and two grand-daughters.